1983

how to read and do proofs

an introduction to mathematical thought process

daniel solow
case western reserve university

1807 1982

john wiley & sons

new york chichester brisbane toronto singapore

*it is hoped that users of this book
will kindly remove and return the questionnaire
included as its last page, to the address that
can be left visible after folding and stapling*

isbn 0 471 86645 8

printed in the united states of america

10 9 8 7 6 5 4 3 2

to my late father . . .

ANATOLE A. SOLOW

and to my mother . . .

RUTH SOLOW

foreword

In a related article, "Teaching Mathematics with Proof Techniques," the author has written, "The inability to communicate proofs in an understandable manner has plagued students and teachers in all branches of mathematics." All of those who have had the experience of teaching mathematics and most of those who have had the experience of trying to learn it must surely agree that acquiring an understanding of what constitutes a sound mathematical proof is a major stumbling block for the student. Many students attempt to circumvent the obstacle by avoiding it—trusting to the indulgence of the examiner not to include any proofs on the test. This collusion between student and teacher may avoid some of the unpleasant consequences—for both student and teacher—of the student's lack of mastery, but it does not alter the fact that a key element in mathematics, arguably its most characteristic feature, has not entered the student's repertoire.

Dr. Solow believes that it is possible to teach the student to understand the nature of a proof by systematizing it. He argues his case cogently with a wealth of detail and example in this pamphlet, and I do not doubt that his ideas deserve attention, discussion, and, above all, experimentation. One of his principal aims is to teach the student how to read the proofs offered in textbooks. These proofs are, to be sure, not presented in a systematic form. Thus, much attention is paid—particularly in the two appendices—to showing the reader how to recognize the standard ingredients of a mathematical argument in an informal presentation of a proof.

There is a valid analogy here with the role of the traditional algorithms in elementary arithmetic.

It is important to acquire familiarity with them and
to understand why they work and to what problems they
could, in principle, be applied. But once all of
this has been learned, one would not slavishly
execute the algorithms in real-life situations (even
in the absence of a calculator!). So, the author
contends, it is with proofs. Understand and analyze
their structure—and then you will be able to read
and understand the more informal versions you will
find in textbooks—and finally you will be able to
create your own proofs. Dr. Solow is not claiming
that mathematicians create their proofs by
consciously and deliberately applying the
"forward-backward method"; he is suggesting that we
have a far better chance of teaching an appreciation
of proofs by systematizing them than by our present,
rather haphazard, procedure based on the hope that
the students can learn this difficult art by osmosis.

One must agree with Dr. Solow that, in this
country, students begin to grapple with the ideas of
mathematical proof far too late in their student
careers—the appropriate stage to be initiated into
these ideas is, in the judgement of many, no later
than eighth grade. However, it would be wrong for
university and college teachers merely to excuse
their own failures by a comforting reference to
defects in the student's precollege education.

Today, mathematics is generally recognized as a
subject of fundamental importance because of its
ubiquitous role in contemporary life. To be used
effectively, its methods must be understood
properly—otherwise we cast ourselves in the roles of
(inefficient) robots when we try to use mathematics,
and we place undue strain on our naturally imperfect
memories. Dr. Solow has given much thought to the
question of how an understanding of a mathematical
proof can be acquired. Most students today do not
acquire that understanding, and Dr. Solow's plan to
remedy this very unsatisfactory situation deserves a
fair trial.

Louis D. Beaumont University Professor   PETER HILTON
Case Western Reserve University
Cleveland, Ohio

to the student

After finishing my undergraduate degree, I began
to wonder why learning theoretical mathematics had
been so difficult. As I progressed through my
graduate work, I realized that mathematics possessed
many of the aspects of a game: a game in which the
rules had been partially concealed. Imagine trying
to play chess before you know how all of the pieces
move! It is no wonder that so many students have had
trouble with abstract mathematics.

This pamphlet describes some of the rules by
which the game of theoretical mathematics is played.
It has been my experience that virtually anyone who
is motivated and who has a knowledge of high school
mathematics can learn these rules. Doing so will
greatly reduce the time (and frustration) involved in
learning abstract mathematics. I hope this pamphlet
serves that purpose for you.

To play chess, you must first learn how the
individual pieces move. Only after these rules have
entered your subconscious can your mind turn its full
attention to the more creative issues of strategy,
tactics, and the like. So it appears to be with
mathematics. Hard work is required in the beginning
to learn the fundamental rules presented in this
pamphlet. In fact, your goal should be to absorb
this material so that it becomes second nature to
you. Then you will find that your mind can focus on
the creative aspects of mathematics. These rules are
no substitute for creativity, and this pamphlet is
not meant to teach creativity. However, I do believe
that it can provide you with the tools needed to
express your creativity. Equally important is the
fact that these tools will enable you to understand
and to appreciate the creativity of others.

TO THE STUDENT

You are about to learn a key part of the mathematical thought process. As you study the material and solve problems, be conscious of your own thought process. Ask questions and seek answers. Remember, the only unintelligent question is the one that goes unasked.

Cleveland, Ohio   DANIEL SOLOW
June 1981

to the instructor

The inability to communicate proofs in an understandable manner has plagued students and teachers in all branches of mathematics. The result has been frustrated students, frustrated teachers, and, oftentimes, a "watered down" course to enable the students to follow at least some of the material, or a test that protects students from the consequences of this deficiency in their mathematical understanding.

One might conjecture that most students simply cannot understand abstract mathematics, but my experience indicates otherwise. What seems to have been lacking is a proper method for explaining theoretical mathematics. In this pamphlet I have developed a method for communicating proofs: a common language that can be taught by professors and understood by students. In essence, this pamphlet categorizes, identifies, and explains (at the student's level) the various techniques that are used repeatedly in virtually all proofs.

Once the students understand the techniques, it is then possible to explain any proof as a sequence of applications of these techniques. In fact, it is advisable to do so because the process reinforces what the students have learned in the pamphlet.

Explaining a proof in terms of its component techniques is not difficult, as is illustrated in the examples of this pamphlet. Before each "condensed" proof is an outline of the proof explaining the methodology, thought process, and techniques that are being used. Teaching proofs in this manner requires nothing more than preceding each step of the proof with an indication of which technique is about to be used, and why.

When discussing a proof in class, I actively involve the students by soliciting their help in choosing the techniques and in designing the proof. I have been pleasantly surprised by the quality of their comments and questions. It has been my experience that once the students become comfortable with the proof techniques, their minds tend to address the more important issues of mathematics, such as why a proof is done in a particular way and why the piece of mathematics is important in the first place. This pamphlet is not meant to teach creativity, but I do believe that it does describe many of the necessary underlying skills whose acquisition will free the student's mind to focus on the creative aspects. I have also found that, by using this approach, it is possible to teach subsequent mathematical material at a much more sophisticated level without losing the students.

In any event, the message is clear. I am suggesting that there are many benefits to be gained by teaching mathematical thought process in addition to mathematical material. This pamphlet is designed to be a major step in the right direction by making abstract mathematics understandable and enjoyable to the students and by providing you with a method for communicating with them.

Cleveland, Ohio   DANIEL SOLOW
June 1981

acknowledgments

For helping to get this work known in the mathematics community, my deepest gratitude goes to Peter Hilton, an outstanding mathematician and educator. I also thank Paul Halmos, whose timely recognition and support greatly facilitated the dissemination of the knowledge of the existence of this pamphlet and teaching method. I am also grateful for discussions with Gail Young and George Polya.

Regarding the preparation of the manuscript, no single person had more constructive comments than Tom Butts. He not only contributed to the mathematical content but also corrected many of the grammatical and stylistic mistakes in a preliminary version. I suppose that I should thank his mother for being an English teacher. I also acknowledge Charles Wells for reading and commenting on the first handwritten draft and for encouraging me to pursue the project further. Many other people made substantive suggestions, including Alan Schoenfeld, Samuel Goldberg, and Ellen Stenson.

Cf all the people involved in this project, none deserve more credit than my students. It is because of their voluntary efforts that this pamphlet has been prepared in such a short time. Thanks especially to John Democko for acting in the capacity of senior editor while concurrently trying to complete his Ph.D. program. Also, I appreciate the help that I received from Michael Dreiling and Robert Wenig in data basing the text and preparing the exercises. Michael has worked on this project almost as long as I have. A special word of thanks goes to Greg Madey for coordinating the second rewriting of the document, for adding useful comments, and in general, for keeping me very organized. His responsibilities have subsequently been assumed by Robin Symes.

In addition, I am grateful to Ravi Kumar for the long hours he spent on the computer preparing the final version of the manuscript, to Betty Tracy and Martha Bognar for their professional and flawless typing assitance, and to Virginia Benade for her technical editing. I am also indebted to my class of 1981 for preparing the solutions to the homeworks.

I acknowledge Mr. Gary Ostedt, the mathematics editor of John Wiley and Sons, for his help in speeding the publication process. Also, I thank the following professors for refereeing the manuscript and for recommending its publication: Alan Tucker, David Singer, Howard Anton, and Ivan Niven.

Last but not least, I am grateful to my wife, Audrey, for her help in proof reading and for her patience during yet another of my projects.

D. S.

contents

CONTENTS

TABLES

DEFINITIONS

how to read and do proofs

an introduction to mathematical thought process

1 *the truth of it all*

The objective of mathematicians is to discover and to communicate certain truths. Mathematics is the language of mathematicians, and a proof is a method of communicating a mathematical truth to another person who also "speaks" the language. A remarkable property of the language of mathematics is its precision. Properly presented, a proof will contain no ambiguity: there will be no doubt as to its correctness. Unfortunately, many proofs that appear in textbooks and journal articles are not presented properly; more appropriately stated, the proofs are presented properly for someone who already knows the language of mathematics. Thus, to understand and/or present a proof, you must learn a new language, a new method of thought. This pamphlet explains much of the basic "grammar" you will need, but as in learning any new language, a lot of practice on your part will be needed to become fluent.

The approach of this pamphlet is to categorize and to explain the various techniques that are used in proofs. One objective is to teach you how to read and how to understand a written proof by identifying the techniques that have been used. Learning to do so will enable you to study almost any mathematical subject on your own, a desirable goal in itself.

A second objective of this pamphlet is to teach you to develop and to communicate your own proofs of known mathematical truths. Doing so requires that you use a certain amount of creativity, intuition, and experience. Just as there are many ways to express the same idea in any language, so are there different proofs for the same mathematical fact. The

1

proof techniques presented here are designed to get you started and to guide you through a proof. Consequently, this pamphlet describes not only how the proof techniques work, but also, when each technique is likely to be used, and why. It is often the case that a correct technique can be chosen based on the very form of the problem under consideration. Therefore, when attempting to create your own proof, learn to select a proof technique consciously before wasting hours trying to figure out what to do. The more aware you are of your thought process, the better it is.

The ultimate objective, however, is to use your newly acquired skills and language to discover and to communicate previously unknown mathematical truths. While the goal is an admirable one, it is extremely difficult to attain. The first step in this direction is to reach the level of being able to read proofs and to develop your own proofs of already known facts. This alone will give you a much deeper and richer understanding of the mathematical universe around you.

The basic material on proof techniques is presented in the next eleven chapters. The twelfth chapter is a complete summary and it is followed by two appendices that illustrate the various techniques with several examples.

The pamphlet is designed to be read by anyone with a good knowledge of high school mathematics. Advanced students who have seen proofs before can read the first two chapters, skip to the summary chapter, and subsequently read the two appendices to see how all of the techniques fit together. The remainder of this chapter explains the types of relationships to which proofs can be applied.

Given two statements A and B, each of which may be either true or false, a fundamental problem of interest in mathematics is to show that if A is true then B is true. A proof is a formal method for accomplishing this task. As you will soon discover, the particular form of A and B can often indicate a way to proceed. Some examples of statements are:

1. Two different lines in a plane are
   either parallel or else they intersect
   in exactly one point.
2. 1 = 0.
3. 3x = 5 and y = 1.
4. x is not > 0.
5. There is an angle t such that
   cos(t) = t.

Observe that statement (1) is always true, (2) is
always false, and statements (3) and (4) can be
either true or false depending on the value of a
variable.

It is perhaps not as obvious that statement (5)
is always true. It therefore becomes necessary to
have some method for "proving" that such statements
are true. In other words, a mathematical proof is a
convincing argument that is expressed in the language
of mathematics. Thus, a proof should contain enough
mathematical detail so as to be convincing to the
person(s) to whom the proof is addressed. For
instance, a proof of statement (5) aimed at
convincing a mathematics professor might consist of
nothing more than Figure 1. On the other hand, a
proof directed toward a high school student would
probably require greater detail, perhaps even the
definition of cosine. It is the lack of sufficient
detail that can often make a proof difficult to read
and to understand. One objective of this pamphlet is
to teach you to decipher these "condensed" proofs
that are likely to appear in textbooks and other
mathematical literature.

In order to do a proof, you must know exactly
what it means to show that "if A is true then B is
true." The statement A is often called the *hypothesis*
and B the *conclusion*. For brevity, the statement "if
A is true then B is true" is shortened to "if A then
B" or simply "A implies B." Mathematicians are often
very lazy when it comes to writing. As such, they
have developed a symbolic "shorthand." For instance,
a mathematician would often write "A => B" instead of
"A implies B." For the most part, textbooks do not
use the symbolic notation, but teachers often do, and
eventually you may find it useful too. Therefore

this document will include the appropriate symbols but will not use them in proofs. A complete list of the symbols can be found in the glossary at the end of this pamphlet.

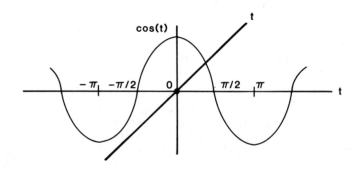

Fig. 1. A proof that there is an angle t such that cos(t) = t.

It seems reasonable that the conditions under which "A implies B" are true will depend on whether A and B themselves are true. Consequently, there are four possible cases to consider:

1. A is true and B is true.
2. A is true and B is false.
3. A is false and B is true.
4. A is false and B is false.

Suppose, for example, that your friend made the statement: "If it rains then Mary brings her umbrella."   Here, the statement A is "it rains" and B is "Mary brings her umbrella." To determine when the statement "A implies B" is false, ask yourself in which of the four cases would you be willing to call your friend a liar. In the first case (i.e., when it does rain and Mary does bring her umbrella) your friend has told the truth. In the second case, it has rained, and yet Mary did not bring her umbrella,

as your friend said she would. Here your friend has
not told the truth. Finally, in cases (3) and (4),
it does not rain. You would not really want to call
your friend a liar in the case of no rain because,
your friend only said that something would happen if
it did rain. Thus, the statement "A implies B" is
true in each of the four cases except the second one,
as summarized in Table 1.

Table 1 is an example of a *truth table*. A truth
table is a method for determining when a complex
statement (in this case, "A implies B") is true by
examining all possible truth values of the individual
statements (in this case, A and B). Other examples
of truth tables will appear in Chapter 3.

According to Table 1, when trying to show that
"A implies B" is true, you can assume that the
statement to the left of the word "implies" (namely
A) is true. Your goal is to conclude that the
statement to the right (namely B) is true. Note that
a proof of the statement "A implies B" is not an
attempt to verify whether A and B themselves are
true, but rather, to show that B is a logical result
of having assumed that A is true.

In general, your ability to show that B is true
will depend very heavily on the fact that you have
assumed A to be true, and ultimately, you will have
to discover the linking relationship between A and B.
Doing so will require a certain amount of creativity
on your part. The proof techniques presented here

Table 1. The Truth of "A Implies B"

****

A	B	A Implies B
True	True	True
True	False	False
False	True	True
False	False	True

****

are designed to get you started and guide you along the path.

Hereafter, A and B will be statements which are either true or false. The problem of interest will be that of showing "A implies B."

Exercises

1.1. Which of the following are statements? (Recall that a statement must be either true or false.)
(a) $ax^2 + bx + c = 0$

(b) $(-b + \sqrt{b^2 - 4ac})/2a$
(c) Triangle XYZ is similar to triangle RST.
(d) $3 + n + n^2$
(e) $\sin(\pi/2) < \sin(\pi/4)$
(f) For every angle t, $\sin^2(t) + \cos^2(t) = 1$.

1.2. For each of the following problems, identify the hypothesis and the conclusion.
(a) If the right triangle XYZ with sides of lengths x and y, and hypotenuse of length z, has an area of $z^2/4$, then the triangle XYZ is isosceles.
(b) n is an even integer => n^2 is an even integer.
(c) If a, b, c, d, e, and f are real numbers with the property that ad - bc ≠ 0, then the two linear equations ax + by = e and cx + dy = f can be solved for x and y.
(d) The sum of the first n positive integers is n(n + 1)/2.
(e) r is real and satisfies $r^2 = 2$ implies r is irrational.
(f) If p and q are positive real numbers with $\sqrt{pq} \neq (p + q)/2$ then p ≠ q.
(g) When x is a real number, the minimum value of x(x - 1) is at least -1/4.

1.3. If you are trying to prove that "A implies B" is true and you know that B is false, do you want to show that A is true or false? Explain.

1.4. Using Table 1, determine the conditions under
which the following statements are true or
false, and give your reason.
(a) If 2 > 7 then 1 > 3.
(b) If 2 < 7 then 1 < 3.
(c) If x = 3 then 1 < 2.
(d) If x = 3 then 1 > 2.

1.5. Prepare a truth table for each of the following
statements.
(a) A implies (B implies C).
(b) (A implies B) implies C.

2 *the forward-backward method*

The purpose of this chapter is to describe one of the fundamental proof techniques: the *forward-backward method*. Special emphasis is given to the material of this chapter because all of the other proof techniques will use the forward-backward method.

The first step in any proof requires recognizing the statements A and B. In general, everything after the word "if" and before the word "then" comprises statement A, while everything after the word "then" constitutes statement B. Alternatively, everything that you are assuming to be true (i.e., the hypothesis) is A; everything that you are trying to prove (i.e., the conclusion) is B. Consider the following example.

Example 1. If the right triangle XYZ with sides of lengths x and y, and hypotenuse of length z, has an area of $z^2/4$, then the triangle XYZ is isosceles (see Figure 2).

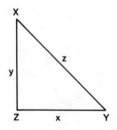

Fig. 2. The right triangle XYZ.

Outline of proof. In this example one has the statements:

> A: The right triangle XYZ with sides of lengths x and y, and hypotenuse of length z has an area of $z^2/4$.
>
> B: The triangle XYZ is isosceles.

Recall that, when proving "A implies B," you can assume that A is true and you must somehow use this information to reach the conclusion that B is true. In attempting to figure out just how to reach the conclusion that B is true, you will be going through a *backward process*. On the other hand, when you make specific use of the information contained in A, you will be going through a *forward process*. Both of these processes will be described in detail.

In the backward process you begin by asking "How or when can I conclude that the statement B is true?" The very manner in which you phrase this question is critical since you must eventually be able to answer it. The question should be posed in an abstract way. For Example 1, the correct abstract question is "How can I show that *a* triangle is isosceles?" While it is true that you want to show that the particular triangle XYZ is isosceles, by asking the abstract question, you call on your general knowledge of triangles, clearing away irrelevant details (such as the fact that the triangle is called XYZ instead of ABC), thus allowing you to focus on those aspects of the problem that really seem to matter. The question obtained from statement B in such problems will be called the *abstraction question*. A properly posed abstraction question should contain no symbols or other notation from the specific problem under consideration. The key to many proofs is formulating a correct abstraction question.

In any event, once you have posed the abstraction question, the next step in the backward process is to answer it. Returning to the example, how can you show that a triangle is isosceles? Certainly one way is to show that two of its sides have equal length. Referring to Figure 2, you should show that $x = y$. Observe that answering the abstraction question is a two phase process. First you give an abstract answer: to show that *a* triangle is isosceles, show that two of *its* sides have equal length. Next, you apply this answer to the specific situation: in this case, to show that two of its sides have equal length means to show that $x = y$, not that $x = z$ or $y = z$. The process of asking the abstraction question, answering it abstractly, and then applying that answer to the specific situation will be referred to as the *abstraction process*.

The abstraction process has given you a new statement, B1, with the property that if you could show that B1 is true then B would be true. For the example above, the new statement is:

B1: $x = y$

If you can show that $x = y$, then the triangle XYZ is isosceles. Once you have the statement B1, all of your efforts must now be directed toward reaching the conclusion that B1 is true, for then it will follow that B is true. How can you show that B1 is true? Eventually you will have to make use of the assumption that A is true, and when solving this problem, you would most likely do so now, but for the moment, let us continue working backward by repeating the abstraction process on the new statement B1. This will illustrate some of the difficulties that can arise in the backward process. Can you pose the new abstraction question?

Since x and y are the lengths of two sides of a triangle, a reasonable abstraction question would appear to be "How can I show that the lengths of two sides of a triangle are equal?" A second perfectly reasonable abstraction question would be "How can I show that two real numbers are equal?" After all, x and y are also real numbers. One of the difficulties that can arise in the abstraction process is the possibility of more than one abstraction question. Choosing the correct one is more of an art than a science. In fortunate circumstances, there will be only one obvious abstraction question. In other cases, you may have to proceed by trial and error. This is where your intuition, insight, creativity, experience, diagrams, and graphs can play an important role. One general guideline is to let the information in A (which you are assuming to be true) help you to choose the question, as will be done in this case.

Regardless of which question you finally settle on, the next step will be to answer it, first in the abstract and then in the specific situation. Can you do this for the two abstraction questions above? For the first one, you might show that two sides of a triangle have equal length by showing that the angles opposite them are equal. For the triangle XYZ of Figure 2, this would mean that you have to show that angle X equals angle Y. A cursory examination of the contents of statement A does not seem to provide much information concerning the angles of triangle XYZ. For this reason, the other abstraction question will be chosen.

Now one is faced with the question "How can I show that two real numbers (namely x and y) are equal?" One answer to this question would be to show that the difference of the two numbers is 0. Applying this answer to the specific statement B1 means you would have to show that $(x - y) = 0$. Unfortunately, there is another perfectly acceptable answer: show that the first number is less than or equal to the second number and also that the second number is less than or equal to the first number. Applying this answer to the specific statement B1, you would have to show that $x \leq y$ and $y \leq x$. Thus, a second difficulty can arise in the backward process. Even if you choose the correct abstraction question, there may be more than one answer to it. Moreover, you might choose an answer that will not permit you to complete the proof. For instance, associated with the abstraction question "How can I show that a triangle is isosceles?" is the answer "Show that the triangle is equilateral." Of course it will be impossible to show that triangle XYZ of Example 1 is equilateral, since one of its angles is 90 degrees.

Returning to the abstraction question "How can I show that two real numbers (namely x and y) are equal?" suppose, for the sake of argument, that you choose the answer of showing that their difference is 0. Once again, the abstraction process has given you a new statement, B2, with the property that if you could show that B2 is true, then in fact P1 would be true, and hence so would B. Specifically, the new statement is:

B2: $x - y = 0$

Now all of your efforts must be directed toward reaching the conclusion that B2 is true. You must ultimately make use of the information in A, but for the moment, let us continue once more with the abstraction process applied to the new statement B2.

One abstraction question is "How can I show that the difference of two real numbers is 0?" At this point it may seem that there is no reasonable answer to this question. Yet another problem can arise in the abstraction process. The abstraction question might have no apparent answer! Do not despair: all is not lost. Remember that when proving "A implies B" you are allowed to assume that A is true. Nowhere have you made use of this fact. It is time to do so through the forward process.

The forward process involves starting with the statement A, which you assume to be true and deriving from it some other statement A1, which you know to be true as a result of A being true. It should be emphasized that the statements derived from A are not haphazard. Rather, they are directed toward linking up with the last statement derived in the backward process. This last statement should act as the guiding light in the forward process. Let us return to Example 1, keeping in mind the fact that the last statement obtained in the backward process was "$x - y = 0$."

For the example above, the statement A is "The right triangle XYZ with sides of length x and y, and hypotenuse of length z, has an area of $z^2/4$." One fact that you know (or should know) as a result of A being true is that $xy/2 = z^2/4$, because the area of a right triangle is one-half the base times the height, in this case $xy/2$. So you have obtained the new statement:

A1: $xy/2 = z^2/4$

Another useful statement follows from A by the Pythagorean theorem, so you also have:

A2: $(x^2 + y^2) = z^2$

The forward process can also combine and use the new statements to produce more true statements. For instance, it is possible to combine A1 and A2 by replacing z^2 in A1 with $(x^2 + y^2)$ from A2 obtaining the statement:

A3: $xy/2 = (x^2 + y^2)/4$

One of the problems with the forward process is that it is also possible to generate some useless statements, for instance, "angle X is less than 90 degrees." While there are no specific guidelines for producing new statements, keep in mind the fact that the forward process is directed toward obtaining the statement B2: $x - y = 0$, which was the last one derived in the backward process. It is for this reason that z^2 was eliminated from A1 and A2.

Continuing with the forward process, you should attempt to rewrite A3 so as to make it look more like B2. For instance, you can multiply both sides of A3 by 4 and subtract 2xy from both sides to obtain:

A4: $(x^2 - 2xy + y^2) = 0$

By factoring you can obtain:

A5: $(x - y)^2 = 0$

One of the most common steps of the forward process is to rewrite statements in different forms, as was done in obtaining A4 and A5. For Example 1, the final step in the forward process (and in the entire proof) is to take the square root of both sides of the equality in A5, thus obtaining precisely the statement B2: $x - y = 0$. The proof is now complete since you started with the assumption that A is true and used it to derive the conclusion that B2, and hence B, is true. The steps and reasons are summarized in Table 2.

It is interesting to note that the forward process ultimately produced the elusive answer to the abstraction question associated with B2: "How can I show that the difference of two real numbers is 0?"—which was to show that the square of the difference is 0 (see A5 in Table 2).

Finally, you should realize that, in general, it will not be practical to write down the entire thought process that goes into a proof, for this would require far too much time, effort, and space. Rather, a highly condensed version is usually presented and often makes little or no reference to the backward process. For the problem above it might go something like this.

Proof of Example 1. From the hypothesis and the formula for the area of a right triangle, the area of XYZ $= xy/2 = z^2/4$. By the Pythagorean theorem, $(x^2 + y^2) = z^2$, and on substituting $(x^2 + y^2)$ for z^2 and performing some algebraic manipulations one obtains $(x - y)^2 = 0$. Hence $x = y$ and the triangle XYZ is isosceles.// (The "//" or some equivalent symbol is usually used to indicate the end of the proof. Sometimes the letters Q.E.D. are used as they stand for the Latin words *quod erat demonstrandum*, meaning "which was to be demonstrated.")

Sometimes the shortened proof will be partly backward and partly forward. For example:

Proof of Example 1. The statement will be proved by establishing that $x = y$, which in turn is done by showing that $(x - y)^2 = (x^2 - 2xy + y^2) = 0$. But the area of the triangle is $(1/2)xy = (1/4)z^2$, so that $2xy = z^2$. By the Pythagorean theorem, $z^2 = (x^2 + y^2)$ and hence $(x^2 + y^2) = 2xy$, or $(x^2 - 2xy + y^2) = 0$, as required.//

Table 2. Proof of Example 1

****

Statement	Reason
A : Area of XYZ is $z^2/4$	Given
A1: $xy/2 = z^2/4$	Area = (base)(height)/2
A2: $x^2 + y^2 = z^2$	Pythagorean theorem
A3: $xy/2 = (x^2 + y^2)/4$	Substitute A2 into A1
A4: $x^2 - 2xy + y^2 = 0$	Algebra
A5: $(x - y)^2 = 0$	Factoring A4
B2: $(x - y) = 0$	Take square root in A5
B1: $x = y$	Add y to both sides of B2
B : XYZ is isosceles	Since B1 is true

****

    The proof can also be written entirely from the backward process. Although this version is slightly unnatural, nonetheless, it is worth seeing.

Proof of Example 1. To reach the conclusion, it will be shown that $x = y$ by verifying that $(x - y)^2 = (x^2 - 2xy + y^2) = 0$, or equivalently, that $(x^2 + y^2) = 2xy$. This can be established by showing that $2xy = z^2$, for the Pythagorean theorem states that $(x^2 + y^2) = z^2$. In order to see that $2xy = z^2$, or equivalently, that $(1/2)xy = (1/4)z^2$, note that $(1/2)xy$ is the area of the triangle and it is equal to $(1/4)z^2$ by hypothesis, thus completing the proof.//

    Proofs found in research articles are often very condensed, giving little more than a hint of how to do the proof. For example:

Proof of Example 1. The hypothesis together with the Pythagorean theorem yield $(x^2 + y^2) = 2xy$, hence $(x - y)^2 = 0$. Thus the triangle is isosceles as required.//

Note that the word "hence" effectively conceals the reason that $(x - y) = 0$. Was it algebraic manipulation (as we know it was) or something else? Unfortunately, these shortened versions are typically given in mathematics books, and it is this fact that makes proofs so hard to read. You should strive toward the ability to read and to dissect a condensed proof. To do so, you will have to figure out which proof technique is being used (since the forward-backward method is not the only one available). Then, from what is written, you will have to discover the thought process that went into the proof and, finally, be able to verify all of the steps involved. The more condensed the proof, the harder this process will be. Some examples of how to read condensed proofs appear in the two appendices. In this pamphlet, your life will be made substantially easier because an outline describing the proof technique, methodology, and reasoning that was involved will precede each condensed proof. Out of necessity, these outlines will be more succinct than the one given in Example 1.

A summary of the forward-backward method for proving "A implies B" is in order. Begin with the statement B, which you are trying to conclude is true. Through the abstraction process of asking and answering the abstraction question, derive a new statement, B1, with the property that if B1 is true, then so is B. All efforts are now directed toward establishing that B1 is true. To that end, apply the abstraction process to B1 obtaining a new statement, B2, with the property that if B2 is true, then so is B1 (and hence B). Remember that the abstraction process is motivated by the fact that A is assumed to be true. Continue in this manner until either you obtain the statement A (in which case the proof is finished) or until you can no longer pose and/or answer the abstraction question fruitfully. In the latter case, it is time to start the forward process, in which you derive a sequence of statements from A that are necessarily true as a result of A being assumed true. Remember that the goal of the forward process is to obtain precisely the last statement you had in the backward process, at which time you will have successfully completed the proof.

The forward and backward processes can easily be remembered by thinking of the statement B as a needle in a haystack. When you work forward from the assumption that A is true, you start somewhere on the outside of the haystack and try to find the needle. In the backward process, you start at the needle and try to work your way out of the haystack toward the statement A (see Figure 3).

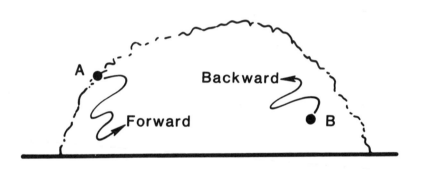

Fig. 3. Finding a needle in a haystack.

Another way of remembering the forward-backward method is to think of a maze in which A is the starting point and B is the desired ending point (see Figure 4). It might be necessary to alternate several times between the forward and backward processes before you succeed, for there are likely to be several false starts and blind alleys.

As a general rule, the forward-backward method
is probably the first technique to try on a problem
unless you have reason to use a different approach
based on the form of B, as will be described shortly.
In any case, you will gain much insight into the
relationship between A and B.

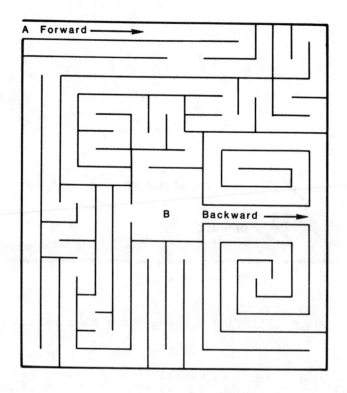

Fig. 4. The maze.

Exercises

Note: All proofs should contain an outline of proof as well as a condensed version.

2.1. Explain the difference between the forward and backward processes. Describe how each one works and what can go wrong. How are the two processes related to each other?

2.2. Consider the problem of proving that "If x is a real number, then the maximum value of $-x^2 + 2x + 1$ is ≥ 2." Which of the following abstraction questions is incorrect, and why?
   (a) How can I show that the maximum value of a parabola is $\geq$ to a number?
   (b) How can I show that a number is $\leq$ to the maximum value of a polynomial?
   (c) How can I show that the maximum value of the function $-x^2 + 2x + 1$ is $\geq$ to a number?
   (d) How can I show that a number is $\leq$ to the maximum of a quadratic function?

2.3. Consider the problem of showing that "If

$$R = \{\text{real numbers } x: x^2 - x \leq 0\},$$
$$S = \{\text{real numbers } x: -(x-1)(x-3) \geq 0\}, \text{ and}$$
$$T = \{\text{real numbers } x: x \geq 1\},$$

then R intersect S is a subset of T." Which of the following is the most correct abstraction question, and why? Explain what is wrong with the other choices.
   (a) How can I show that a set is a subset of another set?
   (b) How can I show that the set R intersect S is a subset of T?
   (c) How can I show that every point in R intersect S is $\geq$ to 1?
   (d) How can I show that the intersection of two sets has a point in common with another set?

2.4. For each of the following problems, list as many abstraction questions as you can (at least two).

Be sure that your questions contain no symbols or notation from the specific problem.

(a) If ℓ_1 and ℓ_2 are the tangent lines to a circle C at the two endpoints e_1 and e_2 of a diameter d, respectively, then ℓ_1 and ℓ_2 are parallel.

(b) If f and g are continuous functions then the function f + g is continuous.
(Note: Continuity is a property of a function.)

(c) If n is an even integer then n^2 is an even integer.

(d) If n is a given integer that satisfies $-3n^2 + 2n + 8 = 0$, then $2n^2 - 3n = -2$.

2.5. For each of the following abstraction questions, list as many answers as you can (at least three).

(a) How can I show that two real numbers are equal?

(b) How can I show that two triangles are congruent?

(c) How can I show that two lines are parallel?

(d) How can I show that a quadrilateral is a rectangle?

2.6. For each of the following problems, (1) pose an abstraction question, (2) answer it abstractly, and (3) apply your answer to the specific problem.

(a) If a, b, and c are real numbers for which $a > 0$, $b < 0$, and $b^2 - 4ac = 0$, then the solution to the equation $ax^2 + bx + c = 0$ is positive.

(b) In the following diagram, if SU is a perpendicular bisector of RT, and $\overline{RS} = 2\overline{RU}$, then triangle RST is equilateral.

2.7. For each of the following hypotheses, list as many statements as you can (at least three) that are a result of applying the forward process for precisely one step.
(a) The real number x satisfies $x^2 - 3x + 2 < 0$.
(b) The sine of angle X in triangle XYZ of Figure 2 is $1/\sqrt{2}$.
(c) The circle C consists of all values for x and y that satisfy $(x - 3)^2 + (y - 2)^2 = 25$.
(d) The triangle UVW is equilateral.

2.8. Consider the problem of proving that "If x and y are real numbers such that $x^2 + 6y^2 - 25 = 0$ and $y^2 + x = 3$, then $|y| = 2$." In working forward from the hypothesis, which of the following is not valid, and why?
(a) $y^2 = 3 - x$
(b) $y^2 = 25/6 - (x/\sqrt{6})^2$
(c) $(3 - y^2)^2 + 6y^2 - 25 = 0$
(d) $(x + 5) = -6y^2/(x - 5)$

2.9. Consider the problem of proving that "If x and y are nonnegative real numbers that satisfy $x + y = 0$, then $x = 0$ and $y = 0$."
(a) For the following condensed proof, write an outline of the proof indicating the forward and backward steps, and the abstraction questions and answers.

Proof. First it will be shown that $x \le 0$, for then, since $x \ge 0$ by the hypothesis, it must be that $x = 0$. To see that $x \le 0$, by the hypothesis, $x + y = 0$, so $x = -y$. Also, since $y \ge 0$, it follows that $-y \le 0$ and hence $x = -y \le 0$. Finally, to see that $y = 0$, since $x = 0$ and $x + y = 0$, it must be that $0 + y = y = 0.//$

(b) Rewrite the condensed proof of part (a) entirely from the backward process.

2.10. Consider an alphabet consisting of the two letters δ and t, together with the following rules for creating new words from old ones. The rules can be applied in any order.

1. Double the current word (e.g., sts could become $stssts$).
2. Erase tt from the current word (e.g., $stts$ could become ss).
3. Replace sss in the current word by t (e.g., $stsss$ could become stt).
4. Add the letter t at the right end of the current word if its last letter is s (e.g., tss could become $tsst$).

(a) Use the forward process to derive all of the possible words that can be obtained in three steps by repeatedly applying the above rules to the initial word s.
(b) Apply the backward process one step to the word tst. Specifically, list all of the words for which an application of one of the above rules would result in tst.
(c) Prove that "If s then tst."
(d) Prove that "If s then $ttst$."

2.11. Prove that if the right triangle XYZ of Figure 2 is isosceles, then the area of the triangle is $z^2/4$.

2.12. Prove that the statement in 2.6(b) is true.

3 on definitions and mathematical terminology

In the previous chapter you learned the forward-backward method and saw the importance of formulating and answering the abstraction question. One of the simplest yet most effective ways of answering an abstraction question is through the use of a definition, as will be explained in this chapter. In addition, you will learn some of the "vocabulary" of the language of mathematics.

A *definition* is nothing more than a statement that is agreed on by all parties concerned. You have already come across a definition in Chapter 1. There we defined what it means for the statement "A implies B" to be true. Specifically, we agreed that it is true in all cases except when A is true and B is false. Nothing says that you must accept this definition as being correct. If you choose not to, then we will be unable to communicate regarding this particular idea.

Definitions are not made randomly. Usually they are motivated by a mathematical concept that occurs repeatedly. In fact, a definition can be viewed as an abbreviation that is agreed on for a particular concept. Take, for example, the notion of "a positive integer greater than one that is not divisible by any positive integer other than one and itself," that is abbreviated (or defined) as a "prime." Surely it is easier to say "prime" than "a positive integer greater than one . . . ," especially if the concept comes up frequently. Several other examples of definitions would be:

23

Definition 1. An integer n divides an integer m (written n|m) if m = kn for some integer k.

Definition 2. A positive integer p > 1 is prime if the only positive integers that divide p are 1 and p.

Definition 3. A triangle is isosceles if two of its sides have equal length.

Definition 4. Two pairs of real numbers (x_1, y_1) and (x_2, y_2) are equal if $x_1 = x_2$ and $y_1 = y_2$.

Definition 5. An integer n is even if and only if its remainder on division by 2 is 0.

Definition 6. An integer n is odd if and only if n = 2k + 1 for some integer k.

Definition 7. A real number r is a rational number if and only if r can be expressed as the ratio of two integers p and q in which the denominator q is not 0.

Definition 8. Two statements A and B are equivalent if and only if "A implies B" and "B implies A."

Definition 9. The statement A AND B (written A $\wedge$ B) is true if and only if A is true and B is true.

Definition 10. The statement A OR B (written A $\vee$ B) is true in all cases except when A is false and B is false.

Observe that the words "if and only if" have been used in some of the definitions, but, in general, "if" tends to be used instead of "if and only if." Some terms, such as "set" and "point," are left undefined. One could possibly try to define a set as a collection of objects, but to do so is impractical because the concept of an "object" is too vague. One would then be led to ask for the definition of an "object," and so on, and so on. Such philosophical issues are beyond the scope of this document.

In the proof of Example 1, a definition was already used to answer an abstraction question. Recall the very first one, which was "How can I show that a triangle is isosceles?" Using Definition 3, in order to show that a triangle is isosceles, one shows that two of its sides have equal length. Definitions are equally useful in the forward process. For instance, if you know that an integer n is odd, then by Definition 6 you would know that n = 2k + 1 for some integer k. Using definitions to work forward and backward is a common occurrence in proofs.

It is often the case that there are two possible definitions for the same concept. Take, for example, the notion of an even integer that was introduced in Definition 5. A second plausible definition for an even integer is "an integer that can be expressed as two times some integer." Of course there can be only one definition for a particular concept, so when more possibilities exist, how do you select the definition and what happens to the other alternatives? Since a definition is simply something agreed on, any one of the alternatives can be agreed on as the definition. Once the definition has been chosen, it would be advisable to establish the "equivalence" of the definition and the alternatives.

For the case of an even integer, this would be accomplished by using Definition 5 to create the statement A: "n is an integer whose remainder on division by 2 is 0." Using the alternative concept, one then creates the statement B: "n is an integer that can be expressed as two times some integer." To establish the fact that the definition is equivalent to the alternative, you must show that "A implies B" and "B implies A" (see Definition 8). Then you would know that if A is true (i.e., n is an integer whose remainder on division by 2 is 0), then B is true (i.e., n is an integer that can be expressed as two times some integer). Moreover, if B is true then A is true too.

The statement that A is equivalent to B is often written "A is true if and only if B is true" or, more simply, "A if and only if B." In mathematical notation one would write "A iff B" or "A <=> B." Whenever you are asked to show that "A if and only if B," you must show that "A implies B" and "B implies A."

It is quite important to be able to establish that a definition is equivalent to an alternative. Suppose, for example, that, in some proof, you derive the abstraction question "How can I show that an integer is even?" As a result of having obtained the equivalence of the two concepts, you now have two possible answers at your fingertips. One is obtained directly from the definition, so one way to show that an integer is even is to show that its remainder on division by 2 is 0. The second answer comes from the alternative: you can show that the integer can be expressed as two times some integer. Similarly, in the forward process, if you know that n is an even integer, then you would have two possible statements that are true as a result of this: the original definition and the alternative. While the ability to answer an abstraction question (or to go forward) in more than one way can be a hindrance, as was the case in Example 1, it can also be advantageous, as shown in the next example.

Example 2. If n is an even integer then n^2 is an even integer.

Outline of proof. Proceeding by the forward-backward method, you are led immediately to the abstraction question "How can I show that an integer (namely n^2) is even?" By choosing the alternative over the definition, you can answer this question by showing that n^2 can be expressed as two times some integer, the only question being which integer. The answer comes from the forward process.

Since n is an even integer, using the alternative, n can be expressed as two times some integer, say k (i.e., n = 2k). So

$$n^2 = (n)(n) = (2k)(2k) = 4k^2 = 2(2k^2).$$

Thus, it has been shown that n^2 can be written as two times some integer, that integer being $2k^2$, and this completes the proof. Of course this problem could also have been solved by using Definition 5, but it is much harder that way.

Proof of Example 2. Since n is an even integer, there is an integer k for which n = 2k. Consequently $n^2 = (2k)^2 = 2(2k^2)$, and so n^2 is an even integer.//

A definition is one common method for working forward and for answering certain abstraction questions. The more statements that you can show are equivalent to the definition, the more ammunition you will have available for the forward and backward processes; however, a large number of equivalent statements can also make it difficult to know exactly which one to use.

In dealing with proofs, there are four terms that you will often come across in mathematics: proposition, theorem, lemma, and corollary. A *proposition* is a true statement of interest that you are trying to prove. All of the examples that have been presented here are propositions. Some propositions are (subjectively) considered to be extremely important and these are referred to as *theorems*. The proof of a theorem can be very long, and it is often easier to communicate the proof in "pieces." For example, in proving the statement "A implies B," it may first be necessary to show that "A implies C," then that "C implies D," and finally that "D implies B." Each of these supporting propositions might be presented separately and would be referred to as a lemma. In other words, a *lemma* is a preliminary proposition that is to be used in the proof of a theorem. Once a theorem has been established, it is often the case that certain propositions follow almost immediately as a result of knowing that the theorem is true. These are called *corollaries*. In summary, a proposition is a true statement that you are trying to prove, and a theorem is an important proposition. Finally, a lemma is a preliminary proposition that is to be used in the proof of a theorem, and a corollary is a proposition that follows from a theorem.

Just as there are certain mathematical concepts that are accepted without a formal definition, so are there certain propositions that are accepted without a formal proof. These unproved propositions are called *axioms*. One example of an axiom is the statement: "the shortest distance between two points is a straight line." A further discussion of axioms is beyond the scope of this document.

Just as a definition can be used in the forward and backward processes, so can a (previously proven) proposition, as will be shown in the next example.

Example 3. If the right triangle RST with sides of lengths r and s, and hypotenuse of length t satisfies $t = \sqrt{2rs}$, then the triangle RST is isosceles (see Figure 5).

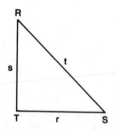

Fig. 5. The right triangle RST.

Outline of proof. The forward-backward method gives rise to the abstraction question "How can I show that a triangle (namely RST) is isosceles?" One answer is to use Definition 3, but a second answer is also provided by the conclusion of Example 1, which states that the triangle XYZ is isosceles. Perhaps the current triangle RST is also isosceles for the same reason as triangle XYZ. In order to find out, it is necessary to see if RST also satisfies the hypothesis of Example 1, as did triangle XYZ, for then RST will also satisfy the conclusion, and hence be isosceles.

In verifying the hypothesis of Example 1 for the triangle RST, it is first necessary to "match up" the current notation with that of Example 1. To be specific, the corresponding lengths are x = r, y = s, and z = t. Thus, to check the hypothesis of Example 1 for the current problem, you must see if the area of triangle RST equals $1/4(t^2)$, or equivalently, since the area of triangle RST is $1/2(rs)$, you must see if $1/2(rs) = 1/4(t^2)$.

The fact that $1/2(rs) = 1/4(t^2)$ will be established by working forward from the current hypothesis that $t = \sqrt{2rs}$. To be specific, on squaring both sides and dividing by 4, one obtains $1/2(rs) = 1/4(t^2)$, as desired. Do not forget to observe that the hypothesis of Example 1 also requires that the triangle RST be a right triangle, which of course it is, as stated in the current hypothesis.

Notice how much more difficult it would have been to match up the notation if the current triangle had been labeled WXY with sides of length w and x, and hypotenuse of length y. Unfortunately this "overlapping" notation can (and will) arise, and, when it does, it is particularly important to keep the symbols straight.

In the condensed proof that follows, note the complete lack of reference to the matching of notation.

Proof of Example 3. By the hypothesis, $t = \sqrt{2rs}$, so $t^2 = 2rs$, or equivalently, $1/4(t^2) = 1/2(rs)$. Thus, the area of the right triangle RST = $1/4(t^2)$. As such, the hypothesis, and hence the conclusion, of Example 1 is true. Consequently, the triangle RST is isosceles.//

Using the conclusion of a previous proposition to answer an abstraction question is quite common. Do not forget that you must match up the current notation to that of the previous proposition so that the hypothesis of the previous proposition can be verified.

Associated with a statement A is the statement NOT A (sometimes written ∼A). The statement NOT A is true when A is false, and vice versa. More will be said about the NOT of a statement in Chapter 10.

Given two statements A and B, you have already learned the meaning of the statement "A implies B." There are many other ways of saying the statement "A implies B," for example:

1. Whenever A is true, B must also be true.
2. B follows from A.
3. B is a necessary consequence of A.
4. A is sufficient for B.
5. A only if B.

Three other statements related to "A implies B" are:

1. "B implies A"   (called the *converse*)
2. "NOT A implies NOT B"   (called the *inverse*)
3. "NOT B implies NOT A"   (called the *contrapositive*)

Table 1 can be used to determine when each of these three statements is true. For instance, the contrapositive statement, "NOT B implies NOT A," is true in all cases except when the statement to the left of the word "implies" (namely NOT B) is true and the statement to the right of the word "implies" (namely NOT A) is false. In other words, the contrapositive statement is true in all cases except when B is false and A is true, as shown in Table 3.

Note, from Table 3, that the statement "NOT B implies NOT A" is true under the same conditions as "A implies B," that is, in all cases except when A is true and B is false. This observation gives rise to a new proof technique known as the contrapositive method that will be described in Chapter 9. Truth tables similar to Table 3 can be derived for the converse and inverse statements and are left as exercises.

This chapter has explained the meaning of many of the terms used in the language of mathematics. More importantly, it showed how definitions and how

Table 3. The Truth Table for "NOT B Implies NOT A"

****

A	B	NOT B	NOT A	A => B	NOT B => NOT A
True	True	False	False	True	True
True	False	True	False	False	False
False	True	False	True	True	True
False	False	True	True	True	True

****

previous propositions can often be used in the forward-backward method. Now it is time to learn more proof techniques.

Exercises

Note: All proofs should contain an outline of proof as well as a condensed version.

3.1. For each of the following conclusions, pose an abstraction question. Then use a definition to (1) answer the question abstractly and (2) apply the answer to the specific problem.
   (a) If n is an odd integer, then n^2 is an odd integer.
   (b) If s and t are rational numbers with $t \neq 0$, then s/t is rational.
   (c) Suppose that a, b, c, d, e, and f are real numbers. If (x_1, y_1) and (x_2, y_2) are real numbers satisfying:

$$ax_1 + by_1 = e, \quad cx_1 + dy_1 = f,$$

$$ax_2 + by_2 = e, \quad cx_2 + dy_2 = f,$$

then (x_1, y_1) equals (x_2, y_2).

(d) If n is a positive integer greater than 1 for which $2^n - 1$ is prime, then n is prime.

(e) If $(n-1)$, n, and $(n+1)$ are three consecutive integers, then 9 divides the sum of their cubes.

3.2. For each of the following hypotheses, use a definition to work forward one step.

(a) If n is an odd integer then n^2 is an odd integer.

(b) If s and t are rational numbers with $t \neq 0$, then s/t is rational.

(c) If triangle RST is equilateral then the area of the triangle is $\sqrt{3}/4$ times the square of the length of a side.

(d) If the right triangle XYZ of Figure 2 satisfies $\sin(X) = \cos(X)$, then triangle XYZ is isosceles.

(e) If a, b, and c are integers for which $a|b$ and $b|c$, then $a|c$.

3.3. Write truth tables for the following statements.

(a) The converse of "A implies B."

(b) The inverse of "A implies B."
How are (a) and (b) related?

(c) A OR B

(d) A AND B

(e) A AND NOT B

(f) (NOT A) OR B
How is (f) related to "A implies B?"

3.4. For each of the following propositions, write down the converse, inverse, and contrapositive statements.

(a) If n is an integer for which n^2 is even then n is even.

(b) If r is a real number such that $r^2 = 2$, then r is not rational.

(c) If the quadrilateral ABCD is a parallelogram with one right angle, then the quadrilateral ABCD is a rectangle.

(d) If t is an angle for which $\sin(t) = \cos(t)$ and $0 < t < \pi$, then $t = \pi/4$.

3.5. Prove that if n is an odd integer, then n^2 is an odd integer.

3.6. Prove that if n is an odd integer and m is an odd integer, then mn is an odd integer.

3.7. Prove that if "A implies B" and "B implies C," then "A implies C."

3.8. Prove that if "A implies B," "B implies C," and "C implies A," then A is equivalent to B and A is equivalent to C.

3.9. Suppose that you have a definition in the form of a statement A together with three possible alternative definitions, say B, C, and D.
   (a) How many proofs would it require to show that A is equivalent to each of the three alternatives?
   (b) How many proofs would it require to show that "A implies B," "B implies C," "C implies D," and "D implies A?"
   (c) Explain why the approach in part (b) is sufficient to establish that each of the alternatives is equivalent to the original definition (and to each other).

3.10. Prove that if the right triangle UVW with sides of lengths u and v, and hypotenuse of length w satisfies $\sin(U) = \sqrt{u/2v}$, then the triangle UVW is isosceles, by:
   (a) Using the definition of an isosceles triangle.
   (b) Verifying the hypothesis of Example 1.
   (c) Verifying the hypothesis of Example 3.

4 quantifiers–I: the construction method

In the previous chapter you saw that a definition could successfully be used to answer an abstraction question. The next four chapters provide you with several other techniques for formulating and answering an abstraction question that arises when B has a special form.

Two particular forms of B appear repeatedly throughout all branches of mathematics. They can always be identified by certain key words that appear in the statement. The first one has the words "there is" ("there are," "there exists"), whereas the second one has "for all" ("for each," "for every," "for any"). These two groups of words are referred to as *quantifiers*, and each one will give rise to its own proof technique. The remainder of this chapter deals with the *existential quantifier* "there is" and with the corresponding proof technique called the *construction method*. The *universal quantifier* "for all" and its associated proof technique is discussed in the next chapter.

The quantifier "there is" arises quite naturally in many mathematical statements. Recall Definition 7 for a rational number as being a real number that can be expressed as the ratio of two integers in which the denominator is not zero. This definition could just as well have been written using the quantifier "there are."

Definition 11. A real number r is rational if and only if there are integers p and q with $q \neq 0$ such that $r = p/q$.

Another such example arises from the alternative definition of an even integer, that being an integer that can be expressed as the product of two times some integer. Using a quantifier to express this statement, one obtains:

Definition 12. An integer n is even if and only if there is an integer k such that n = 2k.

It is important to observe that the quantifier "there is" allows for the possibility of more than one such object, as is shown in the next definition.

Definition 13. An integer n is a square if there is an integer k such that $n = k^2$.

Note that if an integer n (say, for example, n = 9) is square, then there are usually two values of k that satisfy $n = k^2$ (in this case, k = 3 or −3). More will be said in Chapter 11 about the issue of uniqueness (i.e., the existence of only one such object).

There are many other instances where an existential quantifier can and will be used, but from the examples above, you can see that such statements always have the same basic structure. Each time the quantifier "there is," "there are," or "there exists" appears, the statement will have the following basic form:

There is an "object" with a "certain property" such that "something happens."

The words in quotation marks depend on the particular statement under consideration, and you must learn to read, to identify, and to write each of the three components. Consider these examples.

1. There is an integer x > 2 such that $(x^2 - 5x + 6) = 0$.
   Object: integer x
   Certain property: x > 2
   Something happens: $(x^2 - 5x + 6) = 0$

2. There are real numbers x and y both > 0 such that
    $(2x + 3y) = 8$ and $(5x - y) = 3$.
    Object: real numbers x and y
    Certain property: $x > 0$, $y > 0$
    Something happens: $(2x + 3y) = 8$ and $(5x - y) = 3$

Mathematicians often use the symbol "∃" to
abbreviate the words "there is" ("there are," etc.)
and the symbol "∋" for the words "such that" ("for
which," etc.). The use of the symbols is illustrated
in the next example.

3. ∃ an angle t ∋ cos(t) = t.
    Object: angle t
    Certain property: none
    Something happens: cos(t) = t

Observe that the words "such that" (or equivalent
words like "for which") always precede the something
that happens. Practice is needed to become fluent at
reading and writing these statements.

During the backward process, if you ever come
across a statement having the quantifier "there is,"
then one way in which you can proceed to show that
the statement is true is through the construction
method. The idea is to construct (guess, produce,
devise an algorithm to produce, etc.) the desired
object. Of course you must show that the object has
the certain property and that the something happens.
How you actually construct the desired object is not
at all clear. Sometimes it will be by trial and
error; sometimes an algorithm can be designed to
produce the desired object. It all depends on the
particular problem, nonethless, the information in
statement A will surely be used to help accomplish
the task. Indeed, the appearance of the quantifier
"there is" strongly suggests turning to the forward
process to produce the desired object. The
construction method was subtly used in Example 2, but
another example will serve to clarify the process.

Example 4. If a, b, c, d, e, and f are real numbers
with the property that $(ad - bc) \neq 0$, then the two
linear equations $(ax + by) = e$ and $(cx + dy) = f$ can
be solved for x and y.

Outline of proof. On starting the backward process, you should recognize that the statement B has the form discussed above, even though the quantifier "there are" does not appear explicitly. Observe that the statement B can be rewritten to contain the quantifier explicitly, for example, "There are real numbers x and y such that $(ax + by) = e$ and $(cx + dy) = f$." Statements containing "hidden" quantifiers occur frequently in problems and you should watch for them.

Proceeding with the construction method, the issue is how to construct real numbers x and y such that $(ax + by) = e$ and $(cx + dy) = f$. If you are clever enough to "guess" that $x = (de - bf)/(ad - bc)$ and $y = (af - ce)/(ad - bc)$, then you are very fortunate, but you must still show that the something happens, in this case, that $(ax + by) = e$ and $(cx + dy) = f$. This, of course, is not hard to do. Also observe that, by guessing these values for x and y, you have used the information in A since the denominators are not 0.

While this "guess and check" approach is perfectly acceptable for producing the desired x and y, it is not very informative as to how these particular values were produced. A more instructive proof would be desirable. For example, to obtain the values for x and y, you could start with the two equations $(ax + by) = e$ and $(cx + dy) = f$. On multiplying the first equation by d and the second one by b and then subtracting the second one from the first one, you obtain $(ad - bc)x = (de - bf)$. If you then use the information in A, it is possible to divide this last equation by $(ad - bc)$ since, by hypothesis, this number is not 0, thus obtaining $x = (de - bf)/(ad - bc)$. A similar process can be used to obtain $y = (af - ce)/(ad - bc)$. Recall here that a proof is a convincing argument. As such, the statement "a similar process can be used to obtain $y = (af - ce)/(ad - bc)$" might not be very convincing to you, in which case a proof directed at you would have to contain the details of how y is obtained. In any event, you must still show that, for these values of x and y, $(ax + by) = e$ and $(cx + dy) = f$, and that will complete the proof.

Proof of Example 4. On multiplying the equation
(ax + by) = e by d, and the equation (cx + dy) = f by
b, and then subtracting the two equations one obtains
(ad − bc)x = (de − bf). By using the hypothesis,
(ad − bc) ≠ 0, and so dividing by (ad − bc) yields
x = (de − bf)/(ad − bc). A similar argument shows
that y = (af − ce)/(ad − bc), and it is not hard to
check that, for these particular values of x and y,
(ax + by) = e and (cx + dy) = f.//

The construction method is not the only
technique available for dealing with statements
having the quantifier "there is," but it often works
and should be considered seriously. To be successful
with the construction method, you must become a
"builder," and use your creative ability to construct
the desired object having the certain property.
Also, you must not forget to show that the something
happens. Your "building supplies" consist of the
information contained in A.

Exercises

Note: All proofs should contain an outline of proof
as well as a condensed version.

4.1. For each of the following statements, identify
the objects, the certain property, and the
something that happens.
(a) In the Himalayas, there is a mountain over
20,000 feet high that is taller than every
other mountain in the world.
(b) There exists an integer x that satisfies
$x^2 − 5x/2 + 3/2 = 0$.
(c) Through a point P not on a line ℓ, there is
a line ℓ' through P parallel to ℓ.
(d) There exists an angle t between 0 and $\pi/2$
such that sin(t) = cos(t).
(e) Between the two real numbers x and y, there
are distinct rational numbers r and s for
which |r − s| < 0.001.

4.2. Reword the following statements using the symbols "∃" and "∋."

(a) A triangle XYZ is isosceles if two of its sides have equal length.

(b) Given an angle t, one can find an angle t' whose tangent is larger than that of t.

(c) At a party of n people, at least two of the people have the same number of friends.

(d) A polynomial of degree n, say $p(x)$, has exactly n complex roots, say $r_1, \ldots, r_n$, for which $p(r_1) = \ldots = p(r_n) = 0$.

4.3. (a) Prove that there is an integer x such that $x^2 - 5x/2 + 3/2 = 0$. Is the integer unique?

(b) Prove that there is a real number x such that $x^2 - 5x/2 + 3/2 = 0$. Is the real number unique?

4.4. Prove that if a, b, and c are integers for which a|b and b|c, then a|c.

4.5. Prove that if s and t are rational numbers and $t \neq 0$, then s/t is a rational number.

5 *quantifiers–II: the choose method*

This chapter develops the *choose method*, a proof technique for dealing with statements containing the quantifier "for all." Such statements arise quite naturally in many mathematical areas, one of which is set theory. Some time will be devoted to this topic right here and now because it will demonstrate the use of the quantifier "for all."

A *set* is nothing more than a collection of items. For example, the numbers 1, 4, and 7 can be thought of as a collection of items and hence they form a set. Each of the individual items is called a *member* or *element* of the set and each member of the set is said to *be in* or *belong to* the set. The set is usually denoted by enclosing the list of its members (separated by commas) in braces. Thus, the set consisting of the numbers 1, 4, and 7 would be written {1,4,7}. To indicate that the number 4 belongs to this set, mathematicians would write "4 ∈ {1,4,7}," where the symbol "∈" stands for the words "is a member of." Similarly, to indicate that 2 is not a member of {1,4,7}, one would write "2 ∉ {1,4,7}."

While it is certainly desirable to make a list of all of the elements in a set, sometimes it is impractical to do so because the list is simply too long. For example, imagine having to write down every integer between 1 and 100,000. When a set has an infinite number of elements (such as the set of real numbers that are greater than or equal to 0) it will actually be impossible to make a complete list, even if you wanted to. Fortunately there is a way to

describe such "large" sets through the use of what is
known as *set builder notation*. It involves using a
verbal and mathematical description for the members
of the set. Consider the example of the set of all
real numbers that are greater than or equal to 0.
One would write S = {real numbers x: x ≥ 0}, where
the ":" stands for the words "such that." Everything
following the ":" is referred to as the *defining
property* of the set. The question that one always
has to be able to answer is "How do I know if a
particular item belongs to the set or not?" To answer
such a question, you need only check if the item
satisfies the defining property. If so, then it is
an element of the set, otherwise it is not. For the
example above, to see if the real number 3 belongs to
S, you simply replace x everywhere by 3 and see if
the defining property is true. In this case 3 does
belong to S because 3 is ≥ 0.

Sometimes part of the defining property appears
to the left of the ":" as well as to the right, and,
when trying to determine if a particular item belongs
to the set, you must be sure to verify this portion
of the defining property too. For example, if
T = {real numbers x ≥ 0: $(x^2 - x - 2) ≥ 0$}, then −1
does not belong to T even though it satisfies the
defining property to the right of the ":". The
reason is that it does not satisfy the defining
property to the left of the ":" since −1 is not ≥ 0.

From a proof theory point of view, the defining
property plays exactly the same role as a definition
did: it is used to answer the abstraction question
"How can I show that an item belongs to a particular
set?" One answer is to check that the item satisfies
the defining property.

While discussing sets, observe that it can
happen that no item satisfies the defining property.
Consider, for example,

{real numbers x ≥ 0: $(x^2 + 3x + 2) = 0$}.

The only real numbers for which $(x^2 + 3x + 2) = 0$ are
x = −1 and x = −2. Neither of these satisfies the
defining property to the left of the ":". Such a set

is said to be *empty,* meaning that it has no members. The special symbol "$\emptyset$" is used to denote the empty set.

To motivate the use of the quantifier "for all," observe that it is usually possible to write a set in more than one way, for example, the sets

$S = \{\text{real numbers } x: (x^2 - 3x + 2) \leq 0\}$ and
$T = \{\text{real numbers } x: 1 \leq x \leq 2\}$,
    where $1 \leq x \leq 2$ means that $1 \leq x$ and $x \leq 2$.

Surely for two sets S and T to be the same, each element of S should appear in T and vice versa. Using the quantifier "for all," a definition can now be made.

Definition 14. A set S is said to be a subset of a set T (written $S \subseteq T$) if and only if for each element x in S, x is in T.

Definition 15. Two sets S and T are said to be equal (written $S = T$) if and only if S is a subset of T and T is a subset of S.

Like any definition, these can be used to answer an abstraction question. The first one answers the question "How can I show that a set (namely S) is a subset of another set (namely T)?" by requiring you to show that for each element x in S, x is also in T. As you will see shortly, the choose method will enable you to "show that for each element x in S, x is also in T." The second definition answers the abstraction question "How can I show that the two sets S and T are equal?" by requiring you to show that S is a subset of T and T is a subset of S.

In addition to set theory, there are many other instances where the quantifier "for all" can and will be used, but, from the above example, you can see that all such statements appear to have the same consistent structure. When the quantifiers "for all," "for each," "for every," or "for any" appear, the statement will have the following basic form (which is similar to the one you saw in the previous chapter):

For every "object" with a "certain property," "something happens."

The words in quotation marks depend on the particular statement under consideration, and you must learn to read, to write, and to identify the three components. Consider these examples.

1. For every angle t, $\sin^2(t) + \cos^2(t) = 1$.
    Object: angle t
    Certain property: none
    Something happens: $\sin^2(t) + \cos^2(t) = 1$

Mathematicians often use the symbol "$\forall$" to abbreviate the words "for all" ("for each," etc.). The use of symbols is illustrated in the next example.

2. $\forall$ real numbers y > 0, $\exists$ a real number x $\ni$ $2^x = y$.
    Object: real numbers y
    Certain property: y > 0
    Something happens: $\exists$ a real number x $\ni$ $2^x = y$

Observe that a comma always precedes the something that happens. Sometimes the quantifier is "hidden," for example, the statement "the cosine of any angle strictly between 0 and $\pi/4$ is larger than the sine of the angle" could be phrased equally well as "for every angle t with $0 < t < \pi/4$, $\cos(t) > \sin(t)$." Practice is needed to become fluent at reading and writing these statements.

During the backward process, if you ever come across a statement having the quantifier "for all" in the form discussed above, then one way in which you might be able to show that the statement is true is to make a list of all of the objects having the certain property. Then, for each one, you could try to show that the something happens. When the list is finite, this might be a reasonable way to proceed. However, more often than not, it will not be practicable because the list is too long, or even infinite. You have already dealt with this type of obstacle in set theory where the problem was overcome by using the defining property to describe the set. Here, the choose method will allow you to circumvent the difficulty.

The choose method can be thought of as a proof machine that, rather than actually checking that the something happens for each and every object having the certain property, has the capability of doing so. If you had such a machine, then there would be no need to check the whole (possibly infinite) list because you would know that the machine could always do so. The choose method shows you how to design the inner workings of the proof machine.

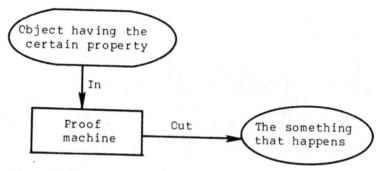

Fig. 6. The proof machine for the choose method.

To understand the mechanics of the choose method, put yourself in the role of the proof machine and keep in mind that you need to have the capability of taking any object with the certain property and concluding that the something happens (see Figure 6). As such, pretend that someone gave you one of these objects, but remember, you do not know precisely which one. All you do know is that the particular object does have the certain property, and you must somehow be able to use the property to reach the conclusion that the something happens. This is most easily accomplished by working forward from the certain property and backward from the something that happens. In other words, with the choose method, you choose one object that has the certain property. Then, by using the forward-backward method, you must conclude that, for the chosen object, the something happens. Then your proof machine will have the capability of repeating the proof for any of the objects having the certain property.

Suppose, for example, that, in some proof, you needed to show that, for all real numbers x with $x^2 - 3x + 2 \leq 0$, $1 \leq x \leq 2$. With the choose method you would choose one of these real numbers, say x', that does have the certain property (in this case, $(x')^2 - 3x' + 2 \leq 0$). Then, by working forward from the fact that $(x')^2 - 3x' + 2 \leq 0$, you must reach the conclusion that, for x', the something happens, that is, $1 \leq x' \leq 2$.

Here, the symbol "x'" has been used to distinguish the chosen object from the general object, "x." This distinction is often ignored (i.e., the same symbol is used for both the general object and the chosen one), and you must be careful to interpret the symbol correctly. Consider the following example.

Example 5. If

$$S = \{\text{real numbers } x: \quad (x^2 - 3x + 2) \leq 0\}, \text{ and}$$

$$T = \{\text{real numbers } x: \quad 1 \leq x \leq 2\},$$

then $S = T$.

Outline of proof. The forward-backward method gives rise to the abstraction question "How can I show that two sets (namely S and T) are equal?" Definition 15 can provide the answer that you must show that S is a subset of T and T is a subset of S, so first try to establish that S is a subset of T, and afterward, that T is a subset of S.

To show that S is a subset of T, you obtain the abstraction question "How can I show that a set (namely S) is a subset of another set (namely T)?" Again, using the definition leads to the answer that you must show that, for all x in S, x is in T. This new statement B1 clearly has the form described above, thus indicating that you should proceed by the choose method. To do so, you must choose an object having the certain property and show that the something happens. In this case that means you should choose an element, say x, in S, and, using the fact that x is in S (i.e., that it satisfies the defining property of S) together with the information in A, you must show that x is in T. Note that you do not want to pick one specific element in S, say 3/2. Also, note the double use of the symbol "x" for both the general and the chosen object.

The statement "x is in T" now becomes B2 and you should apply the abstraction process to B2, obtaining the abstraction question "How can I show that an item (namely x) belongs to a set (namely T)?" together with the answer that you must show that x satisfies the defining property of T (i.e., that $1 \leq x \leq 2$), to which your efforts must be directed.

Turning now to the forward process, you can make use of the information in A to show that $1 \leq x \leq 2$, because you have assumed that A is true. However, there is additional information available to you. Recall that, during the backward process, you made use of the choose method, at which time you chose x to be an element in S. Now is the time to use the fact that x is in S—specifically, since x is in S, from the defining property of the set S, one has $(x^2 - 3x + 2) \leq 0$. Then, by factoring, one obtains $(x - 2)(x - 1) \leq 0$. The only way that the product of the two numbers $(x - 2)$ and $(x - 1)$ can be ≤ 0 is for one of them to be ≤ 0 and the other ≥ 0. In other words, either $(x - 2) \geq 0$ and $(x - 1) \leq 0$, or else $(x - 2) \leq 0$ and $(x - 1) \geq 0$. The first situation can never happen because if it did, x would be ≥ 2 and x would be ≤ 1, which is impossible. Thus the second condition must happen (i.e., $x \leq 2$ and $x \geq 1$), but this is precisely the last statement obtained in the backward process, and hence it has successfully been shown that S is a subset of T. Do not forget that you still have to show that T is a subset of S in order to complete the proof that S = T. This part will be left as an exercise.

Observe that, when you use the choose method, you obtain additional information that is added to the assumption that A is true. Invariably, in the forward process, you will use the extra information.

Proof of Example 5. To show that S = T it will be shown that S is a subset of T and T is a subset of S.

To see that S is a subset of T, let x be in S (the use of the word "let" frequently indicates that the choose method has been invoked). Consequently, $(x^2 - 3x + 2) \leq 0$, and so one has $(x - 2)(x - 1) \leq 0$. This means that either $(x - 2) \geq 0$ and $(x - 1) \leq 0$, or else, $(x - 2) \leq 0$ and $(x - 1) \geq 0$. The former cannot happen because if it did, $x \geq 2$ and $x \leq 1$. Hence it must be that $x \leq 2$ and $x \geq 1$, which means that x is in T. The proof that T is a subset of S is omitted.//

The choose method is a viable approach for dealing with a statement that contains the quantifier "for all." Proceed by choosing an object having the certain property. Add this information to that in A and attempt to show that the something happens by using the forward-backward method.

Exercises

Note: All proofs should contain an outline of proof as well as a condensed version.

5.1. For each of the following definitions, identify the objects, the certain property, and the something that happens.
   (a) The real number x^* is a maximum of the function f if, for every real number x, $f(x) \leq f(x^*)$.
   (b) Suppose that f and g are functions of one variable. Then g is $\geq$ f on the set S of real numbers if, for every element x in S, $g(x) \geq f(x)$.
   (c) The real number u is an upper bound for a set S of real numbers if, for all x in S, $x \leq u$.
   (d) The real number u is a least upper bound for a set S of real numbers if u is an upper bound for S and $\forall$ real numbers $\varepsilon > 0$, $\exists\, x \in S \ni x > u - \varepsilon$.

(e) The set C of real numbers is convex if, for every element x and y in C and for every real number t between 0 and 1, tx + (1 − t)y is an element of C.

(f) The function f of one variable is a convex function if, for all real numbers x and y and for all real numbers $0 \le t \le 1$, it follows that
$$f(tx + (1 - t)y) \le tf(x) + (1 - t)f(y).$$

(g) The function f of one variable is continuous at the point x if, for every real number $\varepsilon > 0$, there is a real number $\delta > 0$ such that, for all real numbers y with $|x - y| < \delta$, $|f(x) - f(y)| < \varepsilon$.

(h) Suppose that $x, x^1, x^2, \ldots$ are real numbers. The sequence $x^1, x^2, \ldots$ converges to x if, $\forall$ real numbers $\varepsilon > 0$, $\exists$ an integer $k' \ni \forall$ integers $k > k'$, $|x^k - x| < \varepsilon$.

5.2. For each of the parts in Exercise 5.1, describe how the choose method would be applied. Use a different symbol to distinguish the chosen object from the general object. For instance, for Exercise 5.1(a), to show that x^* is the maximum of the function f, one would choose a real number, say x', for which it must then be shown that $f(x') \le f(x^*)$. Thus, to apply the choose method in Exercise 5.1(a), one would say "Let x' be a real number. It will be shown that $f(x') \le f(x^*)$."

5.3. Consider the problem of showing that "For every object x with a certain property, something happens." Discuss why the approach of the choose method is the same as that of using the forward-backward method to show that "If x is an object with the certain property, then the something happens." How are the two statements in quotation marks related?

5.4. Reword the following statements using the appropriate symbols $\forall$, $\exists$, $\ni$ wherever necessary.

(a) Some mountain is taller than every other mountain.

(b) If t is an angle then it follows that $\sin(2t) = 2\sin(t)\cos(t)$. (Hint: Make use

of Exercise 5.3.)
(c) The square root of the product of any two nonnegative real numbers p and q is always ≤ their sum divided by 2.
(d) If x and y are real numbers such that x < y, then there is a rational number r such that x < r < y.

5.5. For each of the following statements, indicate which proof techniques you would use (choose and/or construction) and in which order. Also, explain how the technique would be applied to the particular problem, that is, what would you construct, what would you choose, etc.
(a) There is a real number M > 0 such that, for all elements x in the set S of real numbers, |x| ≤ M.
(b) For all real numbers M > 0, there is an element x in the set S of real numbers such that |x| > M.
(c) ∀ real numbers ε > 0, ∃ a real number δ > 0 ∋ ∀ real numbers x and y with |x − y| < δ, |f(x) − f(y)| < ε (where f is a function of one variable).

5.6. For the sets S and T of Example 5, prove that T ⊆ S.

5.7. Prove that for every real number x > 2, there is a real number y < 0 such that x = 2y/(1 + y).

5.8. Prove that if m and b are real numbers, and f is a function defined by f(x) = mx + b, then f is convex. (Hint: Use the definition in Exercise 5.1(f).)

6 *quantifiers–III: induction*

In the previous chapter you learned how to use the choose method when the quantifier "for all" appears in the statement B. There is one very special form of B for which a separate proof technique known as *mathematical induction* has been developed. Induction should seriously be considered (even before the choose method) when B has the form:

For every integer n ≥ 1, "something happens"

where the something that happens is some statement that depends on the integer n. An example would be the statement:

For all integers $n \geq 1$, $\sum_{k=1}^{n} k = n(n+1)/2$,

where $\sum_{k=1}^{n} k = 1+\ldots+n$.

When considering induction, the key words to look for are "integer" and " ≥ 1."

One way to attempt proving such statements would be to make an infinite list of problems, one for each of the integers starting from n = 1, and then prove each statement separately. While the first few problems on the list are usually easy to verify, the issue is how to check the nth one and beyond. For the example above, the list would be:

$P(1)$: $\sum_{k=1}^{1} k = 1(1+1)/2$ or $1 = 1$

$$P(2) \quad : \quad \sum_{k=1}^{2} k \; = \; 2(2+1)/2 \qquad \text{or} \qquad 1+2 \; = \; 3$$

$$P(3) \quad : \quad \sum_{k=1}^{3} k \; = \; 3(3+1)/2 \qquad \text{or} \qquad 1+2+3 \; = \; 6$$

.
.
.

$$P(n) \quad : \quad \sum_{k=1}^{n} k \; = \; n(n+1)/2$$

$$P(n+1): \quad \sum_{k=1}^{n+1} k \; = \; (n+1)[(n+1) + 1]/2 \; = \; (n+1)(n+2)/2$$

.
.
.

Induction is a clever method for proving that each of these statements in the infinite list is true. As with the choose method, induction can be thought of as an automatic problem-solving machine that starts with $P(1)$ and works its way progressively down the list proving each statement as it proceeds. Here is how it works. You start the machine by verifying that $P(1)$ is true, as can easily be done for the example above. Then you feed $P(1)$ into the machine. It uses the fact that $P(1)$ is true and automatically proves that $P(2)$ is true. You then take $P(2)$ and put it into the machine. Once again, it uses the fact that $P(2)$ is true to reach the conclusion that $P(3)$ is true, and so on (see Figure 7). Observe that, by the time the machine is going to prove that $P(n+1)$ is true, it will already have shown that $P(n)$ is true (from the previous step). Thus, in designing the machine, you can assume that $P(n)$ is true, and your job is to make sure that $P(n+1)$ will also be true. Do not forget that, in order to start the whole process, you must also verify that $P(1)$ is true.

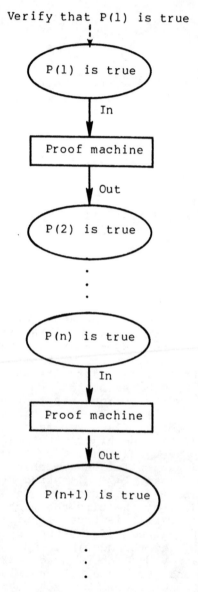

Fig. 7. The proof machine for induction.

To repeat, a proof by induction consists of two steps. The first step is to verify that the statement P(1) is true. To do so, you simply replace n everywhere by 1. Usually, to verify that the resulting statement is true, you will only have to do some minor rewriting.

The second step is much more challenging. It requires that you reach the conclusion that P(n+1) is true by using the assumption that P(n) is true. There is a very standard way of doing this. Begin by writing down the statement P(n+1). Since you are allowed to assume that P(n) is true and you want to conclude that P(n+1) is true, you should somehow try to rewrite the statement P(n+1) in terms of P(n)—as will be illustrated in a moment—for then you will be able to make use of the assumption that P(n) is true. On establishing that P(n+1) is true, the proof will be complete.

Example 6. For every integer $n \geq 1$, $\displaystyle\sum_{k=1}^{n} k = n(n+1)/2$

Outline of proof. When you are using the method of induction, it is helpful to write down the statement P(n), in this case:

$$P(n): \quad \sum_{k=1}^{n} k = n(n+1)/2$$

The first step in a proof by induction is to verify P(1). Replacing n everywhere by 1 in P(n), you obtain

$$P(1): \quad \sum_{k=1}^{1} k = 1(1+1)/2$$

With a small amount of rewriting, it is easy to verify this statement since

$$\sum_{k=1}^{1} k = 1 = 1(1+1)/2$$

This step is often so easy that it is virtually
omitted in the condensed proof by simply saying "The
statement is clearly true for n = 1."

The second step is more involved. You must use
the assumption that P(n) is true to reach the
conclusion that P(n+1) is true. The best way to
proceed is to write down the statement P(n+1) by
carefully replacing n with (n+1) everywhere in P(n),
and rewriting a bit, if necessary. In this case

$$P(n+1): \sum_{k=1}^{n+1} k = (n+1)[(n+1)+1]/2 = (n+1)(n+2)/2$$

To reach the conclusion that P(n+1) is true, begin
with the left side of the equality in P(n+1) and try
to make it look like the right side. In so doing,
you should use the information in P(n) by relating
the left side of the equality in P(n+1) to the left
side of the equality in P(n), for then you will be
able to use the right side of the equality in P(n).
In this example,

$$\sum_{k=1}^{n+1} k = (\sum_{k=1}^{n} k) + (n+1)$$

Now you can use the assumption that P(n) is true by
replacing

$$\sum_{k=1}^{n} k$$

with n(n+1)/2, obtaining

$$\sum_{k=1}^{n+1} k = [n(n+1)/2] + (n+1)$$

All that remains is a bit of algebra to rewrite
[n(n+1)/2 + (n+1)] as [(n+1)(n+2)/2], thus obtaining
the right side of the equality in P(n+1). The
algebraic steps are:

$$n(n+1)/2 + (n+1) = (n^2 + n)/2 + 2(n+1)/2$$

$$= (n^2 + 3n + 2)/2$$

$$= (n+1)(n+2)/2$$

In summary,

$$1+...+(n+1) = (1+...+n) + (n+1)$$

$$= n(n+1)/2 + (n+1)$$

$$= (n^2 + 3n + 2)/2$$

$$= (n+1)(n+2)/2$$

Your ability to relate $P(n+1)$ to $P(n)$ so as to use the induction hypothesis that $P(n)$ is true will determine the success of the proof by induction. If you are unable to relate $P(n+1)$ to $P(n)$, then you might wish to consider a different proof technique.

Proof of Example 6. The statement is clearly true for $n = 1$. Assume that it is true for n (i.e., that $1+...+n = n(n+1)/2$). Then

$$1+...+(n+1) = (1+...+n) + (n+1)$$

$$= n(n+1)/2 + 2(n+1)/2$$

$$= (n^2 + 3n + 2)/2$$

$$= (n+1)(n+2)/2$$

which is $P(n+1)$.//

When using the method of induction, it is not necessary that the first value for n has to be 1. For instance, the statement "for all integers $n \geq 5$, $2^n > n^2$" can also be proved by induction. The only modification is that, in order to start the proof machine, you must verify $P(n)$ for the first possible value of n. In this case, that first value would be $n = 5$, so you will have to check that $2^5 > 5^2$ (which, of course, it is since $2^5 = 32$ while $5^2 = 25$). The second step of the induction proof would remain the same. You would still have to show that if $P(n)$ is true (i.e., $2^n > n^2$), then $P(n+1)$ is also true (i.e., $2^{n+1} > (n+1)^2$). In so doing, you can also use the fact that $n \geq 5$, if necessary.

Another modification to the basic induction method arises when you are having difficulty relating $P(n+1)$ to $P(n)$. Suppose, however, that you can relate $P(n+1)$ to $P(j)$, where $j < n$. In this case, you would like to use the fact that $P(j)$ is true, but can you assume that $P(j)$ is, in fact, true? The answer is yes! To see why, recall the anology of the proof machine, and observe that, by the time the machine has to show that $P(n+1)$ is true, it will already have established that all of the statements $P(1),\ldots,P(j),\ldots,P(n)$ are true (look again at Figure 7). Thus, when trying to show that $P(n+1)$ is true, you can assume that $P(n)$ and all of the preceding statements are true. Such a proof is referred to as *generalized induction*.

Induction is a very powerful technique when applicable; however, it is important to realize that induction does not help you to discover the correct form of the statement $P(n)$. Induction only verifies that a given statement $P(n)$ is true for all integers $n \geq$ some initial one. The key to its success rests in your ability to relate $P(n+1)$ to $P(n)$ or to some previous statement, but do not forget to verify that the statement is also true for the very first possible value of n.

Exercises

Note: Proofs in this chapter need not contain an
      outline of proof.

6.1. For which of the following statements would induction be directly applicable? When it is not applicable, explain why.
(a) For every positive integer n, 8 divides $5^n + 2 \cdot 3^{n-1} + 1$.
(b) There is an integer n ≥ 0 such that $2n > n^2$.
(c) For every integer n ≥ 1, it follows that $1(1!)+...+n(n!) = (n+1)! - 1$. (Recall that $n! = n(n-1)...1.$)
(d) For every integer n ≥ 4, $n! > n^2$.
(e) For every real number n ≥ 1, $n^2 \geq n$.

6.2. (a) Why and when would you want to use induction instead of the choose method?
(b) Why is it not possible to use induction on statements of the form: For every "object" with a "certain property," "something happens?"

6.3. Prove, by induction, that, for every integer n ≥ 1, $1(1!)+...+n(n!) = (n+1)! - 1$.

6.4. Prove, by induction, that, for every integer n ≥ 5, $2^n > n^2$.

6.5. Prove, by induction, that a set of n ≥ 1 elements has 2^n subsets (including the empty set).

6.6. Prove, without using induction, that, for any integer n ≥ 1, $1+...+n = n(n+1)/2$.

6.7. Prove that for every integer n ≥ 1, 6 divides $n^3 - n$, by showing that (1) the statement is true for n = 1, and (2) if the statement is true for (n-1), then it is also true for n.

6.8. Describe a "modified" induction procedure that could be used to prove statements of the form:
(a) For every integer ≤ some initial one, something happens.
(b) For every integer, something happens.
(c) For every positive odd integer, something happens.

6.9. What is wrong with the following proof that   all
horses have the same color?

Proof. Let n be   the   number   of   horses.   When
n = 1,   the   statement is clearly true, that is,
one horse has the same color, whatever color   it
is.   Assume   that any group of n horses has the
same color.   Now   consider   a   group   of   (n+1)
horses.   Taking   any   n   of them, the induction
hypothesis states that they all   have   the   same
color,   say   brown.   The only issue is the color
of the remaining "uncolored"   horse.   Consider,
therefore,   any   other   group   of n of the (n+1)
horses   that   contains   the   uncolored   horse.
Again,   by   the induction hypothesis, all of the
horses in the   new   group   must   have   the   same
color.   Then, since all of the colored horses in
this group are brown, the uncolored   horse   must
also be brown.//

7 quantifiers—IV: specialization

In the previous three chapters you discovered how to proceed when a quantifier appeared in the statement B. This chapter will develop a method for exploiting quantifiers that appear in the statement A. When the statement A contains the quantifier "there is" in the standard form:

There is an "object" with a "certain property" such that "something happens"

you can use this information in a straightforward way. When showing that "A implies B" by the forward-backward method, you are assuming A is true, and in this case that means you can assume that indeed there is an object with the certain property such that the something happens. In doing the proof, you would say: "Let x be an object with the certain property and for which the something happens . . . ." The existence of this object will somehow be used in the forward process to obtain the conclusion that B is true.

The more interesting situation occurs when the statement A contains the quantifier "for all" in the standard form:

For all "objects" with a "certain property," "something happens."

To use this information, one typical method emerges and it is referred to as *specialization*. As a result of assuming A is true, you know that, for all objects with the certain property, something happens. If, at some point in the backward process, you were to come across one of these objects that does have

the certain property, then you can use the
information in A by being able to conclude that, for
this particular object, the something does indeed
happen, and that should help you to conclude that B
is true. In other words, you will have specialized
the statement A to one particular object having the
certain property. For instance, if you know that,
for every angle t, $\sin^2(t) + \cos^2(t) = 1$, then, in
particular, for one angle, say t = $\pi/4$, you can
conclude that $\sin^2(\pi/4) + \cos^2(\pi/4) = 1$. An example
demonstrates the proper use of specialization.

Definition 16. A real number u is an upper bound for
a set of real numbers T if for all
elements t in T, t ≤ u.

Example 7. If R is a subset of a set S of real
numbers and u is an upper bound for S, then u is an
upper bound for R.

Outline of proof. The forward-backward method gives
rise to the abstraction question "How can I show that
a real number (namely u) is an upper bound for a set
of real numbers (namely R)?" Definition 16 is used to
answer the question. Thus, it must be shown that,
for all elements r in R, r ≤ u. The appearance of
the quantifier "for all" in the backward process
suggests proceeding with the choose method, whereby
one chooses an element, say r, in R for which it must
be shown that r ≤ u.

Turning now to the forward process, you will see
how specialization is used to obtain the desired
conclusion that r ≤ u. From the hypothesis that R is
a subset of S, and by Definition 14, you know that
each element in R is also in S. In the backward
process you came across the particular element r in
R, and hence you can use specialization to conclude
that r is in S.

Also, from the hypothesis, you know that u is an
upper bound for S. By Definition 16 this means that,
for every element s in S, s ≤ u. Again, the
appearance of the quantifier "for every" in the
forward process suggests using specialization. In

particular, r is an element of S, as was shown in the previous paragraph. So, by specialization, you can conclude that $r \leq u$. Since the statement "$r \leq u$" was the last one obtained in the backward process, the proof is now complete.

Note that, when using specialization, you must be very careful to keep your notation and symbols in order. Also, be sure that the particular object to which you are specializing does satisfy the certain property, for only then can you conclude that the something happens.

In the condensed proof that follows, note the lack of reference to the forward-backward, choose, and specialization methods.

Proof of Example 7. To show that u is an upper bound for R, let r be an element of R (the word "let" indicates that the choose method has been used). By hypothesis, R is a subset of S and so r is also an element of S (here is where specialization has been used). Furthermore, by hypothesis, u is an upper bound for S, thus, every element in S is $\leq u$. In particular, r is an element of S, so $r \leq u$ (again specialization has been used).//

This and the previous three chapters have provided various techniques for dealing with quantifiers that can appear in either A or B. As always, let the form of the statement guide you. When B contains the quantifier "there is," the construction method can be used to produce the desired object. The choose method is associated with the quantifier "for all," except when the statement B is supposed to be true for every integer starting from some initial one. In the latter case, induction is likely to be successful, provided that you can relate the statement for $(n+1)$ to the one for n. Finally, if the quantifier "for all" appears in the statement A, specialization can often be exploited. When using specialization, be sure that the particular object under consideration does satisfy the certain property, for only then will the something happen.

All of the material thus far has been organized around the forward-backward method. Now it is time to see some other techniques for showing that "A implies B."

Exercises

Note: All proofs should contain an outline of proof as well as a condensed version.

7.1. Explain the difference between the choose and the specialization methods.

7.2. For each of the following statements and given objects, what properties must the object satisfy in order to be able to apply specialization, and, given that it does satisfy the properties, what can you conclude about the object?
(a) Statement: $\forall$ integers $n \geq 5$, $2^n > n^2$.
    Given object: m
(b) Statement: For every element x in the set S with $|x| < 5$, x is in the set T.
    Given object: y
(c) Statement: $\forall$ $\varepsilon > 0$, $\exists \delta > 0 \ni \forall$ y with $|x - y| < \delta$, $|f(x) - f(y)| < \varepsilon$ (where δ, ε, x, and y are real numbers, and f is a function of one variable).
    Given object: ε'
(d) Statement: Any rectangle whose area is one-half the square of the length of a diagonal is a square.
    Given object: the quadrilateral ÇRST
(e) Statement: For any angle t with $0 < t < \pi/4$, $\cos(t) > \sin(t)$.
    Given object: Angle S of the triangle RST

7.3. Prove that if R is a subset of S and S is a subset of T, then R is a subset of T.

7.4. Prove that if S and T are convex sets (see Exercise 5.1(e)), then S intersect T is a convex set.

7.5. Prove that if f is a convex function of one variable (see Exercise 5.1(f)), then for all real numbers $s \geq 0$, the function sf is convex (where the value of the function sf at any point x is $sf(x)$).

7.6. Prove that if f is a convex function of one variable (see Exercise 5.1(f)) and y is a real number, then the set $C = \{$real numbers x: $f(x) \leq y\}$ is convex.

7.7. Prove that 1 is a least upper bound of the set $S = \{1 - 1/2, \quad 1 - 1/3, \quad 1 - 1/4, \ldots \}$ (see Exercise 5.1(d)). (Hint: The set S can be written as $\{$real numbers x: there is an integer $n \geq 2$ such that $x = 1 - 1/n\}$.)

8 *the contradiction method*

As powerful as the forward-backward method is, you may well find yourself unable to complete a proof for one reason or another, as is shown in the next example.

Example 8. If n is an integer and n^2 is even, then n is even.

Outline of proof. The forward-backward method gives rise to the abstraction question "How can I show that an integer (namely n) is even?" One answer is to show that there is an integer k such that n = 2k. The appearance of the quantifier "there is" suggests proceeding with the construction method, and so the forward process will be used in an attempt to produce the desired integer k.

Working forward from the hypothesis that n^2 is even, there is an integer, say m, such that $n^2 = 2m$. Since the objective is to produce an integer k for which n = 2k, it is natural to take the square root of both sides of the equation $n^2 = 2m$ to obtain n = $\sqrt{2m}$, but how can you rewrite $\sqrt{2m}$ to look like 2k? It would seem that the forward-backward method has failed!

Proof of Example 8. The technique that you are about to learn will lead to a simple proof of this problem, and it is left as an exercise.//

Fortunately, there are several other techniques that you might want to try before you give up. In this chapter, the *contradiction method* is described together with an indication of how and when it should be used.

With the contradiction method, you begin by assuming that A is true, just as you would in the forward-backward method. However, to reach the desired conclusion that B is true, you proceed by asking yourself a simple question: "Why can't B be false?" After all, if B is supposed to be true, then there must be some reason why B cannot be false. The objective of the contradiction method is to discover that reason. In other words, the idea of a proof by contradiction is to assume that A is true and B is false, and see why this cannot happen. So what does it mean to "see why this cannot happen?" Suppose, for example, that as a result of assuming that A is true and B is false (hereafter written as NOT B), you were somehow able to reach the conclusion that $0 = 1$!?! Would that not convince you that it is impossible for A to be true and B to be false simultaneously? Thus, in a proof by contradiction, you assume that A is true and that NOT B is true, and, somehow, you must use this information to reach a contradiction to something that you absolutely know to be true.

Another way of viewing the contradiction method is to recall that the statement "A implies B" is true in all cases except when A is true and B is false. In a proof by contradiction, you rule out this one unfavorable case by actually assuming that it does happen, and then reaching a contradiction.

At this point, several very natural questions arise:

1. What contradiction should you be looking for?
2. Exactly how do you use the assumption that A is true and B is false to reach the contradiction?
3. Why and when should you use this approach instead of the forward-backward method?

The first question is, by far, the hardest to answer because there are no specific guidelines. Each problem gives rise to its own contradiction, and it usually takes creativity, insight, persistence, and luck to produce a contradiction.

Method	Assume	Conclude

```
                          forward              backward
Forward-              A}---------> . . . <-----------B
Backward


Contra-             A⎫  forward
diction               ⎬---------> . . . *(contradiction)
              NOT   B⎭
```

Fig. 8. Forward-Backward method versus
contradiction method.

As to the second question, one common approach
to finding a contradiction is to work forward from
the assumption that A and NOT B are true, as will be
illustrated in a moment.

The discussion above also indicates why you
might wish to use contradiction instead of the
forward-backward method. With the forward-backward
method you only assume that A is true, while in the
contradiction method, you can assume that both A and
NOT B are true. Thus, you get two statements from
which to reason forward instead of just one (see
Figure 8). On the other hand, you have no definite
knowledge of where the contradiction will arise.

As a general rule, use contradiction when the
statement NOT B gives you some useful information.
There are at least two recognizable instances when
the contradiction method should be considered.
Recall the statement B associated with Example 8: "n
is an even integer." Obviously an integer can only be
odd or even. When you assume that B is not true
(i.e., that n is not an even integer), then it must
be the case that n is an odd integer. Here, the
statement NOT B has given you some useful
information. In general, when the statement B is one
of two possible alternatives (as in Example 8), the
contradiction method is likely to be effective
because, by assuming NOT B, you will know that the

other case must happen, and that should help you to
reach a contradiction.

A second instance when the contradiction method
is likely to be successful is when the statement B
contains the word "not," as is shown in the next
example.

Example 9. If r is a real number such that $r^2 = 2$,
then r is irrational.

Outline of proof. It is important to note that the
conclusion of Example 9 can be rewritten so as to
read "r is not rational," and as such, the appearance
of the word "not" now suggests using the
contradiction method, whereby you can assume that A
and NOT B are both true. In this case, that means
you can assume that $r^2 = 2$ and that r is a rational
number. Using this information, a contradiction must
now be reached.

Working forward and using Definition 7 for a
rational number, there are integers p and q with
$q \neq 0$ such that $r = p/q$. There is still the
unanswered question of where the contradiction
arises, and this takes a lot of creativity. A
crucial observation here will really help. It is
possible to assume that p and q have no common
divisor (i.e., no integer that divides both p and q),
for if they did, you could divide this integer out of
both the numerator p and the denominator q. Now a
contradiction can be reached by showing that 2 is a
common divisor of p and q! This will be done by
showing that p and q are even, and hence 2 divides
them both.

Working forward, since $r = p/q$, it follows that
$r^2 = p^2/q^2$. But, from the hypothesis, you also know
that $r^2 = 2$, so $2 = p^2/q^2$. The rest of the forward
process is mostly rewriting $2 = p^2/q^2$ via algebraic
manipulations to reach the desired conclusion that
both p and q are even integers. Specifically, upon
multiplying both sides of the last equation by q^2 you
obtain $2q^2 = p^2$. From $2q^2 = p^2$, you can certainly
say that $2q^2$ is even no matter what kind of integer q
is, and since $p^2 = 2q^2$, p^2 must also be even.

Continuing with the forward process, what useful information can be derived from the fact that p^2 is even? Well, the only way for the integer p times itself to be even is for p to be even, and this was the desired conclusion. Recall, once again, that a proof is supposed to be a convincing argument, and this last sentence might not convince you that p is even. In this case it would be necessary to provide more details. As always, a proof should be written with the audience in mind. If you need further convincing that p is even, look at Example 8.

Meanwhile, it is still necessary to show that q is even too. Continuing with the forward process, since p is even, by the alternative definition of an even integer, there is an integer k such that p = 2k. Now, recalling that $2q^2 = p^2$, it follows that $2q^2 = (2k)^2 = 4k^2$, which says that $q^2 = 2k^2$. Once again, $2k^2$ is even no matter what type of integer k is, and since $q^2 = 2k^2$, q^2 is even. Finally, note that the only way for an integer q times itself to be even is for q to be even (see Example 8). Thus, both p and q are even and the desired contradiction has been reached.

Proof of Example 9. Assume, to the contrary, that r is a rational number of the form p/q (where p and q are integers with q ≠ 0) and that $r^2 = 2$. Furthermore, it can be assumed that p and q have no common divisor for, if they did, this number could be canceled from both the numerator p and the denominator q. Since $r^2 = 2$ and r = p/q, it follows that $2 = p^2/q^2$, or equivalently, $2q^2 = p^2$. Noting that $2q^2$ is even, p^2, and hence p, must be even. Consequently, there is an integer k such that p = 2k. On substituting this value for p, one obtains $2q^2 = p^2 = (2k)^2 = 4k^2$, or equivalently, $q^2 = 2k^2$. From this it then follows that q^2, and hence q, must be even. Thus it has been shown that both p and q are even and have the common divisor 2. This contradiction establishes the claim.//

This proof was discovered in ancient times by a follower of Pythagoras, and it epitomizes the use of contradiction. Try to prove the statement by some other method!

There are several other valuable uses for the contradiction method. Recall that, when the statement B contains the quantifier "there is," the construction method is recommended in spite of the difficulty of actually producing the desired object. The contradiction method opens up a whole new approach. Instead of showing that there is an object with the certain property such that the something happens, why not proceed from the assumption that there is no such object? Now your job is to use this information to reach some kind of contradiction. How and where the contradiction arises is not at all clear, but it may be a lot easier than producing or constructing the object. Consider the following example.

Imagine that you wish to show that there are at least two people in the world who have exactly the same number of hairs on their heads. If the construction method is used, then you would actually have to go out and find two such people. To save you the time and trouble, contradiction can be used. In so doing, you can assume that no two people have the same number of hairs on their heads, or equivalently, that everyone has a different number of hairs on their heads. Now, assign numbers to the people in such a way that the person with the fewest hairs receives number 1, the person with the next fewest hairs receives number 2, and so on. Recall that each person is assumed to have a different number of hairs. Thus, the person whose number is 2 must have at least one more hair than the person whose number is 1, and so on. Consequently, the person whose number is one billion must have at least one billion more hairs than the person whose number is 1! Clearly no person can have a billion more hairs than someone else, and so a contradiction has been established.

This example illustrates a subtle but very significant difference between a proof using the construction method and one that uses contradiction. If the construction method is successful, then you will have produced the desired object, or at least indicated how it might be produced, perhaps with the aid of a computer. On the other hand, if you

establish the same result by contradiction, then you
will know that the object exists but will have no way
of physically constructing it. For this reason, it
is often the case that proofs done by contradiction
are quite a bit shorter and easier than those done by
construction because you do not have to create the
desired object. You only have to show that its
nonexistence is impossible! This difference has led
to some great philosophical debates in mathematics.
Moreover, an active area of current research consists
of finding constructive proofs where previously only
proofs by contradiction were known.

As you have seen, the contradiction method can
be a very useful technique when the statement B
contains the word "not" in it. You work forward from
the assumption that A and NOT B are true to reach a
contradiction. One of the disadvantages of the
method is that you do not know exactly what the
contradiction is going to be. The next chapter
describes another proof technique in which you
attempt to reach a very specific contradiction. As
such, you will have a "guiding light" since you will
know what contradiction you are looking for.

Exercises

Note: All proofs should contain an outline of proof
as well as a condensed version.

8.1. When applying the contradiction method to the
following propositions, what should you assume?
(a) If ℓ, m, and n are 3 consecutive integers,
then 24 does not divide $\ell^2 + m^2 + n^2 + 1$.
(b) If the matrix M is not singular then the
rows of M are not linearly dependent.
(c) If f and g are two functions such that (1)
$g \geq f$ and (2) f is unbounded above, then g
is unbounded above.

8.2. Reword each of the following statements so that
the word "not" appears explicitly.
(a) There are an infinite number of primes.
(b) The set S of real numbers is unbounded.
(c) The only positive integers that divide the
positive integer p are 1 and p.
(d) The lines ℓ and ℓ' are parallel.
(e) The real number x is < 5.

8.3. Prove, by contradiction, that if n is an integer
and n^2 is even, then n is even.

8.4. Prove, by contradiction, that no chord of a
circle is longer than a diameter.

8.5. Prove, by contradiction, that if ℓ_1 and ℓ_2 are
two lines in a plane that are both perpendicular
to a third line ℓ in the plane, then ℓ_1 and ℓ_2
are parallel.

8.6. Prove, by contradiction, that, at a party of
$n(\geq 2)$ people, there are at least two people who
have the same number of friends at the party.

8.7. Prove, by contradiction, that there do not exist
three consecutive positive integers such that
the cube of the largest is equal to the sum of
the cubes of the remaining two.

8.8. Prove, by contradiction, that there are an
infinite number of primes. (Hint: Assume that
n is the largest prime. Then consider any prime
number p that divides n! + 1. How is p related
to n?)

8.9. For each of the following statements, indicate
which proof techniques you would use, and in
which order. Specifically, state what you would
assume and what you would try to conclude.
(Note: Throughout, S and T are sets of real
numbers, and all of the variables refer to real
numbers.)
(a) $\exists\ s \in S \ni s \in T$.
(b) $\forall$ s in S, $\nexists$ t in T such that s > t.
(c) $\nexists$ M > 0 such that, $\forall$ x in S, $|x| < M$.

9 *the contrapositive method*

The previous chapter described the contradiction method in which you work forward from the two statements A and NOT B to reach some kind of contradiction. In general, the difficulty with this method is that you do not know what the contradiction is going to be. As will be seen in this chapter, the *contrapositive method* has the advantage of directing you toward one specific type of contradiction.

The contrapositive method is similar to contradiction, in that you begin by assuming that A and NOT B are true. Unlike contradiction however, you do not work forward from both A and NOT B. Instead, you work forward only from NOT B. Your objective is to reach the contradiction that A is false (hereafter written NOT A). Can you ask for a better contradiction than that? How can A be true and false at the same time?

To repeat, in the contrapositive method, you assume that A and NOT B are true and you work forward from the statement NOT B to reach the contradiction that A is false. As such, the contrapositive method can be thought of as a more "passive" form of contradiction in the sense that the assumption that A is true passively provides the contradiction. In the contradiction method however, the assumption that A is true is actively used to reach a contradiction (see Figure 9).

From Figure 9 you can also see the advantages and disadvantages of the contrapositive method over the contradiction method. The disadvantage of the

72

contrapositive method is that you work forward from only one statement (namely NOT B) instead of two. On the other hand, the advantage is that you know precisely what you are looking for (namely NOT A). Because of this, you can often apply the abstraction process to the statement NOT A in an attempt to work backward. The option of working backward is not available in the contradiction method because you do not know what contradiction you are looking for.

Method	Assume	Conclude

Contra-positive
A
forward   backward
NOT B}----------> . . . <----------NOT A

Contra-diction
A⎫ forward
 ⎬----------> . . . *(contradiction)
NOT B⎭

Fig. 9. Contrapositive method versus contradiction method.

The next example demonstrates the contrapositive method.

Example 10. If p and q are positive real numbers such that $\sqrt{pq}$ is not equal to $(p+q)/2$, then p is not equal to q.

Outline of proof. The appearance of the word "not" in the conclusion should suggest using either the contradiction or contrapositive method. Here, the contrapositive method will be used, whereby you will work forward from the statement NOT B and backward from the statement NOT A. In this case, NOT B is the statement "p = q" while NOT A is "$\sqrt{pq} = (p+q)/2$." The objective is to work forward from the fact that p = q to reach the desired conclusion that $\sqrt{pq} = (p+q)/2$. Try to do this for yourself.

Since you want to conclude that $\sqrt{pq} = (p+q)/2$ and you are assuming that p = q, why not replace q everywhere by p? In other words, since p = q, $\sqrt{pq} = \sqrt{pp} = \dot{p}$, and also (p+q)/2 = (p+p)/2 = p. Thus, working forward from the assumption that p = q, it is easy to see that $\sqrt{pq} = (p+q)/2 = p$. Note that the assumption that p > 0 was used in claiming that $\sqrt{pp} = p$.

In the following condensed version of the proof, note that nowhere in the proof does it formally say that the statement NOT A has been reached.

Proof of Example 10. Assume, to the contrary, that p = q. Since p is positive, it then follows that

$$\sqrt{pq} = \sqrt{pp} = p = (p+p)/2 = (p+q)/2$$

and the proof is complete.//

It is also quite interesting to compare the contrapositive and forward-backward methods. In the forward-backward method you work forward from A and backward from B, while in the contrapositive method, you work forward from NOT B and backward from NOT A (see Figure 10).

If you understand Figure 10, then it is not hard to see why the contrapositive method might be better than the forward-backward method. Perhaps you can obtain more useful information by working NOT B forward rather than A. Also, it might be easier to perform the abstraction process on the statement NOT A rather than on B, as would be done in the forward-backward method.

The forward-backward method arose from considering what happens to the truth of "A implies B" when A is true and when A is false (recall Table 1). The contrapositive method arises from similar considerations regarding B. Specifically, if B is true, then according to Table 1, the statement "A implies B" is true. Hence, there is no need to consider the case when B is true. So suppose B is false. In order to ensure that "A implies B" is true, according to Table 1, you would have to show that   A

Method	Assume		Conclude

```
Forward-            forward              backward
Backward      A}---------->   . . .   <----------B


Contra-       A
positive           forward              backward
           NOT B}---------->   . . .   <----------NOT A
```

Fig. 10. Forward-Backward method versus
contrapositive method.

is false. Thus, the contrapositive method has you
assume that B is false and try to conclude that A is
false.

   Indeed, the statement "A implies B" is logically
equivalent to "NOT B implies NOT A" (see Table 3).
As such, the contrapositive method can be thought of
as the forward-backward method applied to the
statement "NOT B implies NOT A." Most condensed
proofs that use the contrapositive method make little
or no reference to the contradiction method.

   In general, it is difficult to know whether the
forward-backward, contradiction, or contrapositive
method will be more effective for a given problem
without trying each one. However, there is one
instance that often indicates that the contradiction
or contrapositive method should be chosen, or at
least considered seriously. This occurs when the
statement B contains the word "not" in it, for then
you will usually find that the statement NOT B has
some useful information.

   In the contradiction method, you work forward
from the two statements A and NOT B to obtain a
contradiction. In the contrapositive method you also
reach a contradiction, but you do so by working
forward from NOT B to reach the conclusion NOT A. You
should also, of course, work backward from NOT A.   A

Method	Assume			Conclude

Forward-
Backward

       forward   backward

A}---------> . . . <---------B

Contra-
diction

    A⎫ forward
      ⎬---------> . . . * (contradiction)
NOT B⎭

Contra-
positive

    A
        forward   backward
NOT B}---------> . . . <---------NOT A

Fig. 11. Forward-Backward method versus
           contradiction method versus
           contrapositive method.

comparison of the forward-backward, contradiction, and contrapositive methods is given in Figure 11.

    Both the contrapositive and contradiction methods require that you be able to write down the NOT of a statement. The next chapter shows you how to do so when the statements contain quantifiers.

Exercises

Note: All proofs should contain an outline of proof as well as a condensed version.

9.1. If the contrapositive method of proof is to be used on the following propositions, then what statement(s) will you work forward from and what statement should you conclude?
(a) If n is an integer for which n^2 is even, then n is even.

(b) Suppose that S is a subset of the set T of real numbers. If S is not bounded then T is not bounded.

(c) If x and y are real numbers with x ≠ y, then f(x) ≠ f(y) (where f is a function of one variable).

(d) If the matrix M is not singular, then the rows of M are not linearly dependent.

9.2. In a proof by the contrapositive method of the proposition "If r is a real number with r > 1, then there does not exist a real number t between 0 and $\pi/4$ such that sin(t) = r cos(t)," which of the following is a result of the forward process?

(a) $r - 1 \leq 0$

(b) $\sin^2(t) = r^2(1 - \sin^2(t))$

(c) $1 - r < 0$

(d) $\tan(t) = 1/r$

9.3. If the contrapositive method is used to prove the proposition "If the derivative of the function f at the point x is not equal to 0, then x is not a local minimum of f," then which of the following is the correct abstraction question? What is wrong with the other choices?

(a) How can I show that the point x is a local minimum of the function f?

(b) How can I show that the derivative of the function f at the point x is 0?

(c) How can I show that a point is a local minimum of a function?

(d) How can I show that the derivative of a function at a point is 0?

9.4. Prove that if c is an odd integer then the equation $n^2 + n - c = 0$ has no odd integer solution for n.

9.5. Suppose that m and b are real numbers with m ≠ 0 and let f be the function that is defined by f(x) = mx + b. Prove that, for all x ≠ y, f(x) ≠ f(y).

9.6. Prove, by the contrapositive method, that if no angle of a quadrilateral RSTU is obtuse, then the quadrilateral RSTU is a rectangle.

10 *nots of nots lead to knots*

As you saw in the previous chapter, the contrapositive method is a valuable proof technique. To use it, however, you must be able to write down the statement NOT B so that you can work it forward. Similarly, you have to know exactly what the statement NOT A is so that you can apply the abstraction process to it. In some instances, the NOT of a statement is easy to find. For example, if A is the statement "the real number x is > 0," then the NOT of A is "it is not the case that the real number x is > 0," or equivalently, "the real number x is not > 0." In fact, the word "not" can be eliminated altogether by incorporating it into the statement to obtain "the real number x is ≤ 0."

A more challenging situation arises when the statement contains quantifiers. For instance, suppose that the statement B contains the quantifier "for all" in the standard form:

> For all "objects" with a "certain property," "something happens."

Then NOT B is the statement:

> It is not the case that, for all "objects" with the "certain property," "something happens"

which really means that there is an object with the certain property for which the something does not happen. Similarly, if the statement B were to contain the quantifier "there is" in the standard form:

There is an "object" with the "certain property"
such that "something happens,"

then NOT B is the statement:

It is not the case that there is an "object" with
the "certain property" such that "something
happens,"

or, in other words, for all objects with the certain
property, the something does not happen.

In general, there are three easy steps to
finding the NOT of a statement containing one or more
quantifiers:

Step 1. Put the word NOT in front of the entire
statement.

Step 2. If the word NOT appears to the left of
a quantifier, then move it to the right
of the quantifier and place it just
before the something that happens. As
you do so, you magically change the
quantifier to its opposite, so that
"for all" becomes "there is" and "there
is" becomes "for all."

Step 3. When all of the quantifiers appear to
the left of the NOT, eliminate the NOT
by incorporating it into the statement
that appears immediately to its right.

These steps will be demonstrated with the following
examples.

1.   For every real number $x \geq 2$, $(x^2 + x - 6) \geq 0$.

Step 1. NOT for every real number $x \geq 2$,
$(x^2 + x - 6) \geq 0$.

Step 2. There is a real number $x \geq 2$ such that
NOT $(x^2 + x - 6) \geq 0$.

Step 3. There is a real number $x \geq 2$ such that
$(x^2 + x - 6) < 0$.

Note in Step 2 that, when the NOT is passed from left to right, the quantifier changes but the certain property (namely $x \geq 2$) does not! Also, since the quantifier "for every" is changed to "there exists," it becomes necessary to replace the "," by the words "such that." In a completely analogous manner, if the quantifier "there exists" is changed to "for all," then the words "such that" are removed and a "," is inserted, as is illustrated in the next example.

2.   There is a real number $x \geq 2$ such that $(x^2 + x - 6) \geq 0$.

    Step 1. NOT there is a real number $x \geq 2$ such that $(x^2 + x - 6) \geq 0$.

    Step 2. For all real numbers $x \geq 2$, NOT $(x^2 + x - 6) \geq 0$.

    Step 3. For all real numbers $x \geq 2$, $(x^2 + x - 6) < 0$.

Finally, if the original statement contains more than one quantifier, then Step 2 will have to be repeated until all of the quantifiers appear to the left of the NOT, as is demonstrated in the next two examples.

3.   For every real number x between −1 and 1, there is a real number y between −1 and 1 such that $(x^2 + y^2) \leq 1$.

    Step 1. NOT for every real number x between −1 and 1, there is a real number y between −1 and 1 such that $(x^2 + y^2) \leq 1$.

    Step 2. There is a real number x between −1 and 1 such that, NOT there is a real number y between −1 and 1 such that $(x^2 + y^2) \leq 1$.

    Step 2. There is a real number x between −1 and 1 such that, for all real numbers y between −1 and 1, NOT $(x^2 + y^2) \leq 1$.

    Step 3. There is a real number x between −1 and 1 such that, for all real numbers y between −1 and 1, $(x^2 + y^2) > 1$.

4. There is a real number x between −1 and 1 such that, for all real numbers y between −1 and 1, $(x^2 + y^2) \leq 1$.

   Step 1. NOT there is a real number x between −1 and 1 such that, for all real numbers y between −1 and 1, $(x^2 + y^2) \leq 1$.

   Step 2. For all real numbers x between −1 and 1, NOT for all real numbers y between −1 and 1, $(x^2 + y^2) \leq 1$.

   Step 2. For all real numbers x between −1 and 1, there is a real number y between −1 and 1 such that NOT $(x^2 + y^2) \leq 1$.

   Step 3. For all real numbers x between −1 and 1, there is a real number y between −1 and 1 such that $(x^2 + y^2) > 1$.

Another situation where you must be careful is in taking the NOT of a statement containing the words AND or OR. Just as the quantifiers are interchanged when taking the NOT of the statement, so the words AND and OR interchange. Specifically, NOT [A AND B] becomes [NOT A] OR [NOT B]. Similarly, NOT [A OR B] becomes [NOT A] AND [NOT B]. For example:

5. NOT [x ≥ 3 AND y < 2] is [x < 3] OR [y ≥ 2].

6. NOT [x ≥ 3 OR y < 2] is [x < 3] AND [y ≥ 2].

Remember that, when you use the contrapositive method of proof, the first thing to do is write down the statements NOT B and NOT A.

Exercises

Note: All proofs should contain an outline of proof as well as a condensed version.

10.1. Write the NOT for each of the definitions in

Exercise 5.1. For instance, 5.1(a) would read "the real number x* is not a maximum of the function f if there is a real number x such that $f(x) > f(x^*)$."

10.2. Reword the following statements so that the word "not" appears explicitly. For example, the statement "$x > 0$" can be reworded to read "x is not ≤ 0."

(a) For each element x in the set S, x is in T.

(b) There is an angle t between 0 and $\pi/2$ such that $\sin(t) = \cos(t)$.

(c) For every "object" with a "certain property," "something happens."

(d) There is an "object" with a "certain property" such that "something happens."

10.3. If the contradiction method is used to prove the following statements, then what should you assume?

(a) For every integer $n \geq 4$, $n! > n^2$.

(b) A implies (B OR C).

(c) A implies (B AND C).

(d) If f is a convex function of one variable, x* is a real number, and there is a real number $\delta > 0$ such that, for all real numbers x that satisfy the property that $|x - x^*| < \delta$, $f(x) \geq f(x^*)$, then for all real numbers y, $f(y) \geq f(x^*)$.

10.4. If the contrapositive method is used to prove each of the following propositions, then what statement(s) will you work forward from and what statement(s) will you work backward from?

(a) A implies (B OR C).

(b) A implies (B AND C).

(c) If n is an even integer and m is an odd integer, then either mn is divisible by 4 or n is not divisible by 4.

10.5. Prove, by contradiction, that if x and y are real numbers such that $x \geq 0$, $y \geq 0$, and $x + y = 0$, then $x = 0$ and $y = 0$.

11 *special proof techniques*

You now have three major proof techniques to help you in proving that "A implies B": the forward-backward, the contrapositive, and the contradiction methods. In addition, when B has quantifiers, you have the choose and construction methods. There are several other special forms of B that have well-established and usually successful proof techniques associated with them. Three of these will be developed in this chapter.

The first is referred to as the *uniqueness method* and it is associated with a statement B that not only wants you to show that there is an object with a certain property such that something happens, but also that the object is unique (i.e., it is the only such object). You will know to use the uniqueness method when the statement B contains the word "unique" as well as the quantifier "there is."

In such a case, your first job is to show that the desired object does exist. This can be done by either the construction or the contradiction method. The next step will be to show uniqueness in one of two standard ways. The first approach has you assume that there are two objects having the certain property and for which the something happens. If there really is only one such object, then, using the certain property, the something that happens, and perhaps the information in A, you must conclude that the two objects are one and the same (i.e., that they are really equal). The forward-backward method is usually the best way to prove that they are equal. The process is illustrated in the next example.

Example 11. If a, b, c, d, e, and f are real numbers such that $(ad - bc) \neq 0$, then there are unique real numbers x and y such that $(ax + by) = e$ and $(cx + dy) = f$.

Outline of proof. The existence of the real numbers x and y was established in Example 4 via the construction method. Here, the uniqueness will be established by the method described above. Thus, you assume that (x_1, y_1) and (x_2, y_2) are two objects with the certain property and for which the something happens. Hence one obtains $a(x_1) + b(y_1) = e$ and $c(x_1) + d(y_1) = f$, and also that $a(x_2) + b(y_2) = e$ and $c(x_2) + d(y_2) = f$. Using these four equations and the assumption that A is true, it will be shown, by the forward-backward method, that the two objects (x_1, y_1) and (x_2, y_2) are equal. Specifically, the abstraction question is "How can I show that two pairs of real numbers (namely (x_1, y_1) and (x_2, y_2)) are equal?" Using the definition of equality of ordered pairs (see Definition 4), one answer is to show that both $x_1 = x_2$ and $y_1 = y_2$, or equivalently, that $(x_1 - x_2) = 0$ and $(y_1 - y_2)^2 = 0$. Both of these statements are obtained from the forward process by applying some algebraic manipulations to the four equations and by using the fact that $(ad - bc) \neq 0$.

Proof of Example 11. The existence of the real numbers x and y was established in Example 4 via the construction method. Hence, only the issue of uniqueness will be addressed. To that end, assume that (x_1, y_1) and (x_2, y_2) are real numbers satisfying

(1) $a(x_1) + b(y_1) = e$,

(2) $c(x_1) + d(y_1) = f$,

(3) $a(x_2) + b(y_2) = e$,

(4) $c(x_2) + d(y_2) = f$.

Subtracting (3) from (1) and (4) from (2) yields

$[a(x_1 - x_2) + b(y_1 - y_2)] = 0$, and

$[c(x_1 - x_2) + d(y_1 - y_2)] = 0$.

On multiplying the first of these equations by d and the second one by b, and then subtracting the second equation from the first one, it follows that $[(ad - bc)(x_1 - x_2)] = 0$. From the hypothesis that $(ad - bc) \neq 0$, one has $(x_1 - x_2) = 0$, and hence $x_1 = x_2$. A similar sequence of algebraic manipulations will establish that $y_1 = y_2$, and thus the uniqueness is proved.//

The second method for showing uniqueness has you assume that there are two different objects having the certain property and for which the something happens. Now supposedly this cannot happen, so, by using the certain property, the something that happens, the information in A, and especially the fact that the objects are different, you must then reach a contradiction. This process is demonstrated in the next example.

Example 12. If r is a positive real number then there is a unique real number x such that $x^3 = r$.

Outline of proof. The appearance of the quantifier "there is" in the conclusion suggests using the construction method to produce a real number x such that $x^3 = r$. This part of the proof will be omitted so that the issue of uniqueness can be addressed. To that end, suppose that x and y are two different real numbers such that $x^3 = r$ and $y^3 = r$. Using this information together with the hypothesis that r is positive, and especially the fact that $x \neq y$, a contradiction will be reached by showing that $r = 0$, thus contradicting the hypothesis that r is positive.

To show that $r = 0$, one can work forward. In particular, since $x^3 = r$ and $y^3 = r$, it follows that $x^3 = y^3$. Thus $(x^3 - y^3) = 0$, and on factoring, one obtains $[(x - y)(x^2 + xy + y^2)] = 0$. Here is where you can use the fact that $x \neq y$ to divide by $(x - y)$, obtaining $(x^2 + xy + y^2) = 0$. Thinking of this as a quadratic equation of the form $(ax^2 + bx + c) = 0$ in which $a = 1$, $b = y$, and $c = y^2$, the quadratic formula states that

$$x = \frac{-y \pm \sqrt{(y^2 - 4y^2)}}{2} = \frac{-y \pm \sqrt{-3y^2}}{2}$$

Since x is real and the above formula for x requires taking the square root of $-3y^2$, it must be that $y = 0$, and if $y = 0$, then $r = y^3 = 0$, and the contradiction has been reached.

Proof of Example 12. Only the issue of uniqueness will be addressed. To that end, assume that x and y are two different real numbers for which $x^3 = r$ and $y^3 = r$. Hence, it follows that $0 = (x^3 - y^3) = [(x - y)(x^2 + xy + y^2)]$. Since $x \neq y$, it must be that $(x^2 + xy + y^2) = 0$. By the quadratic formula, it follows that

$$x = \frac{-y \pm \sqrt{(y^2 - 4y^2)}}{2} = \frac{-y \pm \sqrt{-3y^2}}{2}$$

Since x is real, it must be that $y = 0$. But then $r = y^3 = 0$, thus contradicting the hypothesis that r is positive.//

Another special proof technique, called the *either/or method*, arises when B is of the form "either C is true, or else D is true" (where C and D are statements). In other words, the either/or method is to be used when trying to show that the statement "A implies C OR D" is true. Applying the forward-backward method, you would begin by assuming A is true and you would like to conclude that either C is true or else D is true. Suppose that you were to make the additional assumption that C is not true. Clearly it had better turn out that, in this case, D is true. Thus, with the either/or method, you can assume that A is true and C is false and you must then conclude that D is true, as is illustrated in the next example.

Example 13. If $x^2 - 5x + 6 \geq 0$, then $x \leq 2$ or $x \geq 3$.

Outline of proof. From the above discussion, you can assume that $(x^2 - 5x + 6) \geq 0$ and $x > 2$. It is your job to conclude that $x \geq 3$. Working forward from the assumption that $(x^2 - 5x + 6) \geq 0$, it follows that $[(x - 2)(x - 3)] \geq 0$. Since $x > 2$, $(x - 2) > 0$, and hence $(x - 3) \geq 0$ (i.e., $x \geq 3$, as desired).

Proof of Example 13. Assume that $(x^2 - 5x + 6) \geq 0$ and $x > 2$. It follows that $[(x - 2)(x - 3)] \geq 0$, and, since $(x - 2) > 0$, it must be that $x \geq 3$ as desired.//

It is worth noting that the either/or method could have been done equally well by assuming that A is true and D is false, and then concluding that C is true. Try this approach on Example 13.

The final proof technique to be developed in this chapter is the *max/min method* that arises in problems dealing with maxima and minima. Suppose that S is a nonempty set of real numbers having both a largest and a smallest member. For a given real number x, you might be interested in the position of the set S relative to the number x. For instance, you might want to prove one of the following statements:

1. All of S is to the right of x (see Figure 12(a)).
2. Some of S is to the left of x (see Figure 12(b)).
3. All of S is to the left of x (see Figure 12(c)).
4. Some of S is to the right of x (see Figure 12(d)).

In mathematical problems these four statements are likely to appear, respectively, as:

(a) $\min\{s: s \text{ is in } S\} \geq x$
(b) $\min\{s: s \text{ is in } S\} \leq x$
(c) $\max\{s: s \text{ is in } S\} \leq x$
(d) $\max\{s: s \text{ is in } S\} \geq x$

The proof technique associated with the first two are discussed here and the remaining two are left as exercises. Nonetheless, the idea behind the max/min technique is to convert the given problem into an equivalent problem containing a quantifier. Then, the appropriate choose or construction method can be used.

Consider, therefore, the problem of determining if the smallest member of S is $\geq x$. An equivalent problem containing a quantifier can be obtained by considering the corresponding statement (1) above. Since "all" of S should be to the right of x, you

need to show that, for all elements s in S, x ≤ s, as
is illustrated in the next example.

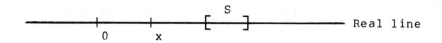

Fig. 12(a). All of S to the right of x.

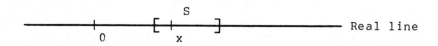

Fig. 12(b). Some of S to the left of x.

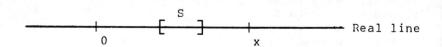

Fig. 12(c). All of S to the left of x.

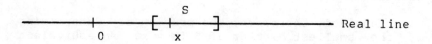

Fig. 12(d). Some of S to the right of x.

Example 14. If R is the set of all real numbers, then
min{x(x - 1): x is in R} ≥ -1/4.

Outline of proof. From the form of B, the max/min
method will be used. As per the discussion above,
the statement B can be converted to "for all real
numbers x, x(x - 1) ≥ -1/4." Once in this form, it
becomes clear that the choose method should be used
to choose a real number x for which it must be shown
that x(x - 1) ≥ -1/4 or, that $(x^2 - x + 1/4) ≥ 0$.
But, since $(x^2 - x + 1/4) = (x - 1/2)^2$, this number
is always ≥ 0, and the proof is complete.

Proof of Example 14. In order to conclude that
min{x(x - 1): x is in R} ≥ -1/4, let x be any real
number. Then it follows that x(x - 1) is ≥ -1/4
because $(x^2 - x + 1/4) = (x - 1/2)^2$, which is ≥ 0.//

Turning now to the problem of showing that the
smallest member of S is ≤ x, the approach is slightly
different. To proceed, consider the corresponding
statement (2) above. Since "some" of S should be to
the left of x, an equivalent problem is to show that
there is an element s in S such that s ≤ x. Then,
the construction or contradiction method could be
used.

This chapter has described three special proof
techniques that are appropriate when B has the
corresponding special form. The final chapter
provides a complete summary.

Exercises

Note: All proofs should contain an outline of proof
as well as a condensed version.

11.1. Prove that if x is a real number that is > 2,
then there is a unique real number y < 0 such
that x = 2y/(1 + y).

11.2. Prove, by using the second uniqueness method, that if m and b are real numbers with $m \neq 0$, then there is a unique number x such that $mx + b = 0$.

11.3. Prove that if a and b are real numbers, at least one of which is not 0, and $i = \sqrt{-1}$, then there is a unique complex number, say $c + di$, such that $(a + bi)(c + di) = 1$.

11.4. What would be the advantages and disadvantages of using the contradiction method instead of the either/or method to prove that "A implies (B OR C)?"

11.5. Prove that if n is an even integer and m is an odd integer, then either 4 divides mn or 4 does not divide n.

11.6. Consider the proposition "If x is a real number that satisfies $x^3 + 3x^2 - 9x - 27 \geq 0$, then $|x| \geq 3$."
(a) Reword the proposition so that it is of the form "A implies B OR C."
(b) Prove the proposition by assuming that A and NOT B are true.
(c) Prove the proposition by assuming that A and NOT C are true.

11.7. Convert the following max/min problems into the appropriate quantifier statement. (Note: S is a set of real numbers and x is a given real number.)
(a) $\max\{s: \ s$ is in $S\} \leq x$
(b) $\max\{s: \ s$ is in $S\} \geq x$
In the remainder of this problem, a, b, c, and u are given real numbers, and x is a variable.
(c) $\min\{cx: \ ax \leq b$ and $x \geq 0\} \leq u$
(d) $\max\{cx: \ ax \geq b$ and $x \geq 0\} \geq u$
(e) $\min\{ax: \ b \leq x \leq c\} \geq u$
(f) $\max\{bx: \ a \leq x \leq c\} \leq u$

11.8. Prove that if S is a nonempty subset of a set T of real numbers and t^* is a real number that satisfies the property that for each element t in T, $t \geq t^*$, then $\min\{s: \ s$ is in $S\} \geq t^*$.

11.9. Suppose that a, b, and c are given real numbers
and that x and u are variables. Prove that
$\min\{cx: ax \geq b, x \geq 0\}$ is at least as large as
$\max\{ub: ua \leq c, u \geq 0\}$.

12 *summary*

The list of proof techniques is now complete.
The techniques presented here are by no means the
only ones, but they do constitute the basic set.
Undoubtedly you will come across others as you are
exposed to more mathematics. Perhaps you will
develop some of your own. In any event, there are
many fine points and tricks that you will pick up
with experience. A final summary of how and when to
use each of the various techniques for proving the
proposition "A implies B" is in order.

With the forward-backward method, you can assume
that A is true and your job is to prove that B is
true. Through the forward process, you will derive
from A a sequence of statements A1, A2, . . . which
are necessarily true as a result of A being assumed
true. This sequence is not random. It is guided by
the backward process whereby, through asking and
answering the abstraction question, you derive from B
a statement, B1, with the property that if it is
true, then so is B. This abstraction process can
then be applied to B1, obtaining a new statement, B2,
and so on. The objective is to link the forward
sequence to the backward sequence by generating a
statement in the forward sequence that is precisely
the same as the last statement obtained in the
backward sequence. Then, like a column of dominoes,
you can do the proof by going forward along the
sequence from A all the way to B. When obtaining the
sequence of statements, watch for quantifiers to
appear, for then the construction, choose, induction,
and/or specialization methods may be useful in doing
the proof.

For instance, when the quantifier "there is" arises in the backward process in the standard form:

There is an "object" with a "certain property" such that "something happens"

you should consider using the construction method to actually produce the desired object. With the construction method, you work forward from the assumption that A is true to construct (produce, or devise an algorithm to produce, etc.) the object. Be sure to check that it satisfies the certain property and also that the something happens.

On the other hand, when the quantifier "for all" arises in the backward process in the standard form:

For all "objects" with a "certain property," "something happens"

you should consider using the choose method. Here, your objective is to design a proof machine that is capable of taking any object with the certain property and proving that the something happens. To do so, you select (or choose) an object that does have the certain property. You must conclude that, for that object, the something happens. Once you have chosen the object, it is best to proceed by working forward from the fact that the chosen object does have the certain property (together with the information in A, if necessary) and backward from the something that happens.

The induction method should be considered (even before the choose method) when the statement B has the form:

For every integer n greater than or equal to some initial one, a statement P(n) is true.

The first step of the induction method is to verify that the statement is true for the first possible value of n. The second step requires you to show that if P(n) is true, then P(n+1) is true. Remember that the success of a proof by induction rests on your ability to relate the statement P(n+1) to P(n)

so that you can make use of the assumption that P(n)
is true. In other words, to perform the second step
of the induction proof, you should write down the
statement P(n), replace n everywhere by (n+1) to
obtain P(n+1), and then see if you can express P(n+1)
in terms of P(n). Only then will you be able to use
the assumption that P(n) is true to reach the desired
conclusion that P(n+1) is also true.

Finally, when the quantifier "for all" arises in
the forward process in the standard form:

For all "objects" with a "certain property,"
"something happens"

you will probably want to use the specialization
method. To do so, watch for one of these objects to
arise in the backward process, for then, by using
specialization, you can conclude that the something
does happen for the particular object that is under
consideration. That fact should then be helpful in
reaching the conclusion that B is true. When using
specialization, be sure to verify that the particular
object does satisfy the certain property, for only
then will the something happen.

When the original statement B contains the word
"not," or when the forward-backward method fails, you
should consider the contrapositive or contradiction
method, with the former being chosen first. To use
the contrapositive approach, you must immediately
write down the statements NOT B and NOT A, using the
techniques of Chapter 10 if necessary. Then, by
beginning with the assumption that NOT B is true,
your job is to conclude that NOT A is true. This is
best accomplished by applying the forward-backward
method, working forward from the statement NOT B and
backward from the statement NOT A. Once again,
remember to watch for quantifiers to appear in the
forward or backward process, for if they do, then the
corresponding construction, choose, induction, and/or
specialization methods may be useful.

In the event that the contrapositive method
fails, there is still hope with the contradiction
method. With this approach, you are allowed to

assume not only that A is true but also that B is false. This gives you two facts from which you must derive a contradiction to something that you know to be true. Where the contradiction arises is not always obvious, but it will be obtained by working the statements A and NOT B forward.

In trying to prove that "A implies B," let the form of B guide you as much as possible. Specifically, you should scan the statement B for certain key words, as they will often indicate how to proceed. For example, if you come across the quantifier "there is," then consider the construction method, whereas the quantifier "for all" suggests using the choose or induction method. When the statement B has the word "not" in it, you will probably want to use either the contrapositive or contradiction method. Other key words to look for are "uniqueness," "either . . . or . . . ," and "maximum" and "minimum," for then you would use the corresponding uniqueness, either/or, and max/min methods. If you are unable to choose an approach based on the form of B, then you should proceed with the forward-backward method. Table 4 provides a complete summary.

You are now ready to "speak" mathematics. Your new "vocabulary" and "grammar" is complete. You have learned the three major proof techniques for proving propositions, theorems, lemmas, and corollaries. They are the forward-backward, contrapositive, and contradiction methods. You have come to know the quantifiers and the corresponding construction, choose, induction, and specialization methods. For special situations, your bag of proof techniques includes the uniqueness, either/or, and max/min methods. If all of these proof techniques fail, you may wish to stick to Greek—after all, it's all Greek to me.

Table 4. Summary of Proof Techniques.

****

Proof Technique	When to Use It	What to Assume
Forward–Backward (page 8)	As a first attempt, or when B does not have a recognizable form	A
Contra-positive (page 72)	When B has the word "not" in it	NOT B
Contra-diction (page 64)	When B has the word "not" in it, or when the first two methods fail	A and NOT B
Construc-tion (page 34)	When B has the term "there is," "there exists," etc.	A
Choose (page 40)	When B has the term "for all," "for each," etc.	A, and choose an object with the certain property
Induction (page 50)	When B is true for each integer beginning with an initial one, say n_0	The statement is true for n

****

****

What to Conclude	How to Do It
B	Work forward from A and apply the abstraction process to B
NOT A	Work forward from NOT B and backward from NOT A
Some contradiction	Work forward from A and NOT B to reach a contradiction
There is the desired object	Guess, construct, etc., the object having the certain property and show that the something happens
That the something happens	Work forward from A and the fact that the object has the certain property. Also work backward from the something that happens.
The statement is true for $n + 1$. Also show it true for n_0.	First substitute n_0 everywhere and show it true. Then invoke the induction hypothesis for n to prove it true for $n + 1$.

****

Table 4. Summary of Proof Techniques (continued).

****

Proof Technique	When to Use It	What to Assume
Special- ization (page 59)	When A has the term "for all," "for each," etc.	A
Unique- ness 1 (page 83)	When B has the word "unique" in it	There are two such objects, and A
Unique- ness 2 (page 85)	When B has the word "unique" in it	There are two different objects, and A
Either/ or 1 (page 86)	When B has the form "C OR D"	A and NOT C
Either/ or 2 (page 87)	When B has the form "C OR D"	A and NOT D
Max/min 1 (page 87)	When B has the form "max $S \leq x$" or "min $S \geq x$"	Choose an s in S, and A
Max/min 2 (page 89)	When B has the form "max $S \geq x$" or "min $S \leq x$"	A

****

****

What to Conclude	How to Do It
B	Work forward by specializing A to one particular object, the one obtained in the backward process
The two objects are equal	Work forward using A and the properties of the objects. Also work backward to show the objects are equal.
Some contradiction	Work forward from A using the properties of the two objects and the fact that they are different
D	Work forward from A and NOT C, and backward from D
C	Work forward from A and NOT D, and backward from C
s ≤ x or s ≥ x	Work forward from A and the fact that s is in S. Also work backward.
Construct s in S so that s ≥ x or s ≤ x	Use A and the construction method to produce the desired s in S

****

Exercises

12.1. For each of the following statements, indicate which proof technique you would use to begin the proof and explain why.

(a) If p and q are odd integers then the equation $x^2 + 2px + 2q = 0$ has no rational solution for x.

(b) For every integer $n \geq 4$, $n! > n^2$.

(c) If f and g are convex functions then $f + g$ is a convex function.

(d) If a, b, and c are real numbers, then the maximum value of $ab + bc + ca$ subject to the condition that $a^2 + b^2 + c^2 = 1$ is ≤ 1.

(e) In a plane, there is one and only one line perpendicular to a given line ℓ through a point P on the line.

(f) If f and g are two functions such that (1) for all real numbers x, $f(x) \leq g(x)$ and (2) there is no real number M such that, for all x, $f(x) \leq M$, then there is no real number $M > 0$ such that, $\forall$ x, $g(x) \leq M$.

(g) If f and g are continuous functions at the point x, then so is the function $f + g$.

(h) If f and g are continuous functions at the point x, then for every real number $\varepsilon > 0$ there is a real number $\delta > 0$ such that, for all real numbers y with $|x - y| < \delta$, $|f(x) + g(x) - (f(y) + g(y))| < \varepsilon$.

(i) If f is a function of one variable defined by $f(x) = 2^x + x^2/2$, then there is a real number x^* between 0 and 1 such that, for all y, $f(x^*) \leq f(y)$.

12.2. Describe how you would use each of the following proof techniques to prove that "for every integer $n \geq 4$, $n! > n^2$". State what you would assume and what you would conclude.

(a) Induction method

(b) Choose method

(c) Forward-Backward method (Hint: Convert the problem to an equivalent one of the form "if . . . then . . . .")

(d) Contradiction method

A *putting it all together–I*

Through the use of a specific example, this appendix will show you how to read and how to understand a written proof as it might appear in a textbook. Subsequently, some general problem-solving strategies will be discussed and demonstrated on a problem.

Due to the way in which most proofs are currently written, it is necessary for you to figure out which proof techniques are being used and why. Often, what makes a written proof so difficult to understand is the fact that the author has omitted part of the thought process, thus forcing you to reconstruct it. Doing so requires that you identify which proof technique is being used and how it applies to the particular problem. The next example demonstrates how to read a proof. Unlike previous examples in this pamphlet, the condensed version of the proof will precede the outline, which then explains how to read the condensed proof.

The example deals with the concept of an "unbounded" set of real numbers, meaning that there are elements in the set that are "arbitrarily" far away from 0. A formal definition of a bounded set will be given first.

Definition 17. A set S of real numbers is bounded if there is a real number M > 0 such that, for all elements x in S, |x| < M.

Example 15. If S is a subset of a set T of real numbers and S is not bounded, then T is not bounded.

Proof of Example 15. (For reference purposes, each sentence of the proof will be written on a separate line.)

S1. Suppose that S is a subset of T and assume to the contrary that T is bounded.

101

S2. Hence there is a real number $M' > 0$ such that, for all x in T, $|x| < M'$.

S3. It will be shown that S is bounded.

S4. To that end, let x' be an element of S.

S5. Since S is a subset of T, it follows that x' is in T.

S6. But then $|x'| < M'$ and so S is bounded, which is a contradiction.//

Outline of proof. An interpretation of each of the statements S1 through S6 will be given.

Interpretation of S1. The author is indicating that the proof is going to be done by contradiction and appropriately is assuming that (part of) A is true, that is, that S is a subset of T, and also that NOT B is true, that is, that T is bounded. Note that the author has not explicitly stated that S is not bounded, although it is being assumed true.

The use of the contradiction method should not come as a surprise since the conclusion of the example contains the word "not." Sometimes it is beneficial to scan through the proof to find the contradiction. In S6 it says that S is bounded, and this contradicts the hypothesis that S is not bounded. Hopefully, statements S2 through S6 will indicate how the author has worked forward from A and NOT B to reach the contradiction.

Interpretation of S2. The author is working forward from the statement NOT B (i.e., that T is a bounded set) via Definition 17 to claim that there is the real number $M' > 0$ such that, for all x in T, $|x| < M'$.

Interpretation of S3. It is here that the author states the desired objective of showing that S is bounded. Observe that there is no indication that the reason for wanting to show that S is bounded is to reach a contradiction.

Interpretation of S4. This statement might seem cryptic at first, and the reason is that the author has omitted several steps of the thought process. What has happened is that the author has implicitly posed the abstraction question "How can I show that a set (namely S) is bounded?" and has then used Definition 17 to answer it, whereby it must be shown that there is a real number M > 0 such that, for all x in S, |x| < M.

Recognizing the quantifier "there is," the construction method should be used to produce the desired value for M. What the author has failed to tell you is that the value for M is M' (see S2). Given that this is the case, it must be shown that M' has the desired properties, i.e., that M' > 0 (which it is) and that, for all x in S, |x| < M'.

Recognizing the appearance of the quantifier "for all" in the backward process, one should then proceed by the choose method. This is precisely what the author has done in S4, where it states: " . . . let x' be an element of S." Once the element x' in S has been chosen, it must then be shown that |x'| < M', which the author has not explicitly said he would do. Observe that the word "let" in S4 indicates that the choose method has been used.

What makes S4 so difficult to understand is the lack of sufficient detail, particularly the omission of the abstraction question and answer, and several other steps. Such details are often left for you to figure out for yourself.

Interpretation of S5. In S5, the author has suddenly switched to the forward process and is working forward from A (i.e., from the fact that S is a subset of T) by using the definition of a subset to conclude that, for all elements x in S, x is in T (see Definition 14). Then, without stating so, the author has specialized this statement to the particular value of x' that is in S, thus concluding that x' is in T. Note once again that part of the author's thought process has been omitted and left for you to figure out. At this point, it is not clear why it is necessary to show that x' is in T.

The reason should be related to showing that
$|x'| < M'$.

Interpretation of S6. It is here that the author
finally concludes that $|x'| < M'$, thus showing that S
is bounded and reaching a contradiction to the
hypothesis that S is not bounded. The only question
is how did the author reach the conclusion that
$|x'| < M'$. Once again, the specific proof technique
has not been mentioned. Actually, the author has
used specialization. Specifically, the statement S2
has been specialized to the particular value of x'.
However, recall that, when using specialization, it
is necessary to verify that the particular object
under consideration (x' in this case) has the certain
property (that x' is in T). The fact that x' is in T
was established in S5, but observe that, at the time,
the author did not tell you why it was being shown
that x' is in T.

Read the condensed proof again. Observe that
what makes it difficult to understand is the lack of
reference to the specific techniques that were used,
especially the abstraction process and the
specialization method. In addition, the author has
omitted part of the thought process. To understand
the proof you have to fill in the missing steps.

In summary, when reading proofs, expect to do
some work of your own. Learn to identify the various
techniques that are being used. Begin by trying to
determine if the forward-backward or contradiction
method is the primary technique. Then try to follow
the methodology associated with that technique. Be
watchful for quantifiers to appear, for then the
corresponding choose, induction, construction, and/or
specialization methods are likely to be used. Be
particularly careful of notational complications that
can arise with the choose and specialization methods.
For instance, in the condensed proof of Example 15,
the author could have used the symbols "x" and "M"
instead of "x'" and "M'." If this had been done, then
you would have had to distinguish between such
statements as "for all x with a certain property,
something happens," in which "x" refers to a general
object, and a statement of the form "let x have a

certain property," in which "x" refers to a specific object. The double use of a symbol is confusing but common in proofs, as is illustrated in the example in Appendix B.

In any event, when you are unable to follow a particular step of a written proof, it is most likely due to the lack of sufficient detail. To fill in the gaps, learn to ask yourself how you would proceed to do the proof. Then try to see if the written proof matches your thought process.

Now that you know how to read a proof, it is time to see how to do a proof on your own. In the example that follows, pay particular attention to how the form of the statement under consideration dictates the technique to be used.

Example 16. If T is a bounded subset of real numbers, then any subset of T is bounded.

Outline of proof. Looking at the statement B, you should recognize the quantifier "for any" and thus you should begin with the choose method. Accordingly, you would write: "Let S be a subset of T. It will be shown that S is bounded." Then the new statement to be proved is:

B1: S is bounded.

Not recognizing any special form to B1, it is probably best to proceed with the forward-backward method. The idea is to work backward from B1 until it is no longer fruitful to do so. Then, the forward process will be applied to the hypothesis that T is a bounded set of real numbers.

Working backward from B1, can you pose an abstraction question? One such question is "How can I show that a set (namely S) is bounded?" A reasonable way to answer an abstraction question is by a definition. Doing so in this case means you must show that:

B2: There is a real number M > 0 such that, for all elements x in S, $|x| < M$.

The appearance of the quantifier "there is" suggests using the construction method and also indicates that you should turn to the forward process to produce the desired value for M. Working forward from the hypothesis that T is bounded, is there anything that you can say is true? At least one possibility is to use the definition, whereby you can conclude that:

A1: There is a real number M' > 0 such that, for all elements x in T, |x| < M'.

Observe that the symbol "M'" has been used instead of "M" because "M" was already used in the backward process.

Perhaps M' is the desired value of M. When using the construction method, it is generally advisable to try to construct the desired object in the most "obvious" way. In this case, that means setting M = M'. If this "guess" is correct, then you must still show that the certain property holds (i.e., M > 0) and also that the something happens (i.e., that for all x in S, |x| < M). It is not hard to see that M > 0 because M' > 0 and M = M'. Thus it remains only to show that:

B3: For all elements x in S, |x| < M.

The appearance of the quantifier "for all" suggests proceeding with the choose method, whereby you would choose an element, say x', in S for which you must show that:

B4: |x'| < M, or, since M = M', |x'| < M'.

Observe that the symbol "x'" has been used for a particular object to avoid confusion with the symbol "x." At this point, it might not be clear how to reach the conclusion that |x'| < M', but look carefully at the statement A1. Observe that you could conceivably use specialization to reach the desired conclusion that |x'| < M', provided that you can specialize the statement to x = x'. In order to be able to do so, you must make sure that the particular object under consideration (namely x') does satisfy the certain property (namely that x' is in T). Your objective, therefore, is to show that x' is in T.

Recall that x' was chosen to be an element of S and that S was chosen to be a subset of T. How can you use this information to show that x' is in T? Working forward from the definition of a subset, you know that, for all x in S, x is in T. Thus, you can specialize this statement to x = x', which you know is in S, and reach the desired conclusion that x' is in T, completing the proof.

Proof of Example 16. Let S be a subset of T. To show that S is bounded, a real number M > 0 will be produced with the property that, for all x in S, |x| < M.

By hypothesis, T is bounded, and so there is a real number M' > 0 such that, for all x in T, |x| < M'. Set M = M'. To see that M has the desired properties, let x' be an element of S. Since S is a subset of T, x' is in T. But then it follows that |x'| < M = M', as desired.//

Problem solving is not a precise science. Some general suggestions will be given here, but a more detailed discussion can be found in George Polya's book <u>How</u> <u>to</u> <u>Solve</u> <u>It</u> (Princeton University Press, Princeton, NJ, 1945) or in Wayne Wickelgren's book <u>How</u> <u>to</u> <u>Solve</u> <u>Problems</u> (W. H. Freeman, San Francisco, CA, 1974).

When trying to prove that "A implies B," consciously choose a technique based on the form of B. If no form is apparent, then it is probably best to proceed with the forward-backward method. If unsuccessful, there are several avenues to pursue before giving up. You might try asking yourself why B cannot be false, thus leading you into the contradiction (or contrapositive) method.

The point is that, when you are unable to complete a proof for one reason or another, it is advisable to seek another proof technique consciously. Sometimes the form of the statement B

can be manipulated so as to induce a different
technique. For instance, suppose that the statement
B contains the quantifier "for all" in the standard
form:

> For all "objects" with a "certain property,"
> "something happens."

If the choose method fails, then you might try
rewriting B so that it reads:

> There is no "object" with the "certain property"
> such that the "something" does not happen.

In this form, the contradiction method suggests
itself because of the appearance of the word "no,"
whereby you would assume that there is an object with
the certain property such that the something does not
happen. Your objective would be to reach a
contradiction.

When the statement B does have a recognizable
form, it is usually best to try the corresponding
proof technique first. Remember that, as you proceed
through a proof, different techniques will be needed
as the form of the statement under consideration
changes.

If you are really stuck, it can sometimes be
advantageous to leave the problem for a while, for
when you return to it, you might see a new approach.
Undoubtedly you will learn many tricks of your own as
you solve more and more problems.

B *putting it all together–II*

This appendix will give you more practice in reading and doing proofs. The examples presented here are more difficult than those in Appendix A. The additional difficulty is due, in part, to the fact that the statements under consideration contain three quantifiers as opposed to two.

The first example is designed to teach you how to read a condensed proof as it might appear in a textbook. As such, the condensed version of the proof will precede the detailed outline which then explains how to read the condensed proof. The example deals with the concept of a "continuous" function of one variable, meaning that if the value of the variable is changed "slightly" then the value of the function does not change "radically." Another way of saying that a function is continuous is that its graph can be drawn without lifting the pencil. To proceed formally, a definition of continuity is given.

Definition 18. A function f of one variable is continuous at the point x if for every real number $\varepsilon > 0$, there is a real number $\delta > 0$ such that, for all real numbers y with the property that $|x - y| < \delta$, it then follows that $|f(x) - f(y)| < \varepsilon$.

Example 17. If f and g are two functions that are continuous at x, then the function f + g is also continuous at x. (Note: The function f + g is the function whose value at any point y is f(y) + g(y)).

Proof of Example 17. (For reference purposes, each sentence of the proof will be written on a separate line.)

S1. To see that the function f + g is continuous at x, let $\varepsilon > 0$.

S2. It will be shown that there is a $\delta > 0$ such that, for all y with $|x - y| < \delta$, $|f(x) + g(x) - (f(y) + g(y))| < \varepsilon$.

S3. Since f is continuous at x, there is a $\delta_1 > 0$ such that, for all y with $|x - y| < \delta_1$, $|f(x) - f(y)| < \varepsilon/2$.

S4. Similarly, since g is continuous at x, there is a $\delta_2 > 0$ such that, for all y with $|x - y| < \delta_2$, $|g(x) - g(y)| < \varepsilon/2$.

S5. Let $\delta = \min\{\delta_1, \delta_2\}$ (which is > 0) and let y have the property that $|x - y| < \delta$.

S6. Then $|x - y| < \delta_1$ and $|x - y| < \delta_2$, and so $|f(x) + g(x) - (f(y) + g(y))| \leq |f(x) - f(y)| + |g(x) - g(y)| < \varepsilon/2 + \varepsilon/2 = \varepsilon$, and the proof is complete.//

Outline of proof. An interpretation of each of the statements S1 through S6 will be given.

Interpretation of S1. This statement indicates that the forward-backward method is going to be used because the statement "to see that $f + g$ is continuous at x" means that the author is about to show that the statement B is true. The question is why did the author say " . . . let $\varepsilon > 0$?" Hopefully it is related to showing that $f + g$ is continuous at x. What has happened is that the author has implicitly posed the abstraction question "How can I show that a function (namely $f + g$) is continuous at a point (namely x)?" and has used Definition 18 to answer it, whereby it must be shown that, for every $\varepsilon > 0$, "something happens."

Recognizing the appearance of the quantifier "for every" in the backward process, one should then proceed with the choose method, whereby a specific value of $\varepsilon > 0$ would be chosen. The author has done this when he says " . . . let $\varepsilon > 0$." Observe that the symbol "ε" appearing in the definition of continuity refers to a general value for ε while the symbol "ε" appearing in S1 refers to a specific value resulting from the choose method. The double use of

a symbol can be confusing but is common in written
proofs.

What makes S1 so difficult to understand is that
the author has omitted part of the thought process,
namely, the abstraction question and answer.   Such
details are often left for you to figure out for
yourself.

Interpretation of S2. The author is stating precisely
what he is going to do, but why should he want to
show that there is a $\delta > 0$ such that "something
happens?" Recall that, in S1, the choose method was
used to select an $\epsilon > 0$ and so, it must be shown
that, for that ϵ, the something happens.   That
something is "there is a $\delta > 0$ . . . " as stated in
S2 (see Definition 18).

Interpretation of S3. The author has turned to the
forward process (having recognized from S2 that the
quantifier "there is" suggests using the construction
method to produce the desired $\delta > 0$). The author is
working forward from the hypothesis that f   is
continuous at x by using Definition 18. What the
author has failed to tell you is that, in the
definition, the quantifier "for all" arises, and the
statement has been specialized to the value of $\epsilon/2$,
where ϵ is the one that was chosen in S1. Note,
again, that the symbol "ϵ" in Definition 18 refers to
a general value for ϵ while the symbol "ϵ" in S1
refers to a specific value for ϵ. At this moment, it
is not clear why the author decided to specialize to
the value of $\epsilon/2$ as opposed to ϵ.   The reason will
become evident in S6.

Interpretation of S4. The author is working forward
from the fact that g is continuous at x in precisely
the same way that was done in S3. Keep in mind that,
from S2, the author is trying to construct a value of
$\delta > 0$ for which something happens.

Interpretation of S5. It is here that the desired
value of $\delta > 0$ is produced. The values of δ_1 and δ_2,
from S3 and S4, respectively, are combined to give
the desired δ, namely, $\delta = \min\{\delta_1, \delta_2\}$. It is not yet
clear why δ has been constructed in this way. In any

event, it is the author's responsibility to show that $\delta > 0$ and also that δ satisfies the desired property that, for all y with $|x - y| < \delta$, $|f(x) + g(x) - (f(y) + g(y))| < \varepsilon$ (see S2).

In S5 the author merely remarks that $\delta > 0$ (which is true because both δ_1 and δ_2 are > 0). Also, the reason that the author has said " . . . let y have the property that $|x - y| < \delta$" is because the choose method is being used to show that, for all y with $|x - y| < \delta$, $|f(x) + g(x) - (f(y) + g(y))| < \varepsilon$. Note, once again, the double use of the symbol "y." Nonetheless, to complete the proof, it must be shown that $|f(x) + g(x) - (f(y) + g(y))| < \varepsilon$.

Interpretation of S6. It is here that the author concludes that $|f(x) + g(x) - (f(y) + g(y))| < \varepsilon$. The only question is how. It is not hard to see that $|f(x) + g(x) - (f(y) + g(y))| \leq |f(x) - f(y)| + |g(x) - g(y)|$ because the absolute value of the sum of two numbers, namely $f(x) - f(y)$ and $g(x) - g(y)$, is always $\leq$ the sum of the absolute values of the two numbers, but why is $|f(x) - f(y)| + |g(x) - g(y)| < \varepsilon/2 + \varepsilon/2$? Once again the author has omitted part of the thought process.

What has happened is that specialization has been used to claim that $|f(x) - f(y)| < \varepsilon/2$ and $|g(x) - g(y)| < \varepsilon/2$. Specifically, statements S3 and S4 have both been specialized to the particular value of y that was chosen in S5. Recall that, when using specialization, one must be sure that the particular object under consideration (namely y) satisfies the certain property (in this particular case, $|x - y| < \delta_1$ and $|x - y| < \delta_2$). Note that, in S6, the author does indeed claim that $|x - y| < \delta_1$ and $|x - y| < \delta_2$, but can you see why this is true? Look again at S5. Since y was chosen so that $|x - y| < \delta$ and $\delta = \min\{\delta_1, \delta_2\}$, it must be that both $\delta \leq \delta_1$ and $\delta \leq \delta_2$, so indeed $|x - y| < \delta_1$ and $|x - y| < \delta_2$. Hence, the author is justified in specializing S3 and S4 to this particular value of y and hence can conclude that $|f(x) - f(y)| < \varepsilon/2$ and $|g(x) - g(y)| < \varepsilon/2$. In other words, the author is justified in claiming that $|f(x) + g(x) - (f(y) + g(y))| \leq |f(x) - f(y)| + |g(x) - g(y)| < \varepsilon/2 + \varepsilon/2 = \varepsilon$. Perhaps now it is also clear why the author specialized (in S3 and S4) to ε/2 instead of ε.

Again, note that what makes S6 so hard to understand is the omission of part of the thought process. You must learn to fill in the missing links by determining which proof technique is being used and consequently what has to be done.

The next example illustrates how to go about doing your own proof. Pay particular attention to how the form of the statement under consideration leads to the correct technique.

Example 18. If f is a function of one variable that, at the point x, satisfies the property that there are real numbers $c > 0$ and $\delta' > 0$ such that, for all y with $|x - y| < \delta'$, $|f(x) - f(y)| \leq c|x - y|$, then f is continuous at x.

Outline of proof. Begin by looking at the statement B and trying to select a proof technique. Since B does not have a particular form, the forward-backward method should be used. Thus, you are led to the abstraction question "How can I show that a function (namely f) is continuous at a point (namely x)?" As usual, a definition is available to provide an answer, that being to show that:

B1: For all $\varepsilon > 0$, there is a $\delta > 0$ such that, for all y with $|x - y| < \delta$, $|f(x) - f(y)| < \varepsilon$.

Looking at B1, you should recognize the quantifier "for all" and hence use the choose method to select a particular value of $\varepsilon > 0$. It is advisable to use a symbol other than "ε" for the specific choice so as to avoid confusion. In the condensed proof you would write "Let $\varepsilon' > 0$ . . . ." Once you have selected $\varepsilon' > 0$, the choose method requires you to show that the something happens, in this case:

B2: There is a $\delta > 0$ such that, for all y with $|x - y| < \delta$, $|f(x) - f(y)| < \varepsilon'$.

Looking at B2, you should recognize the

quantifier "there is" and hence use the construction method to produce the desired value of δ. When the construction method is used, it is advisable to turn to the forward process to produce the desired object.

Working forward from the hypothesis that there are real numbers $c > 0$ and $\delta' > 0$ for which something happens, you should attempt to construct δ. Perhaps $\delta = \delta'$ (or perhaps $\delta = c$). Why not "guess" that $\delta = \delta'$ and see if it is correct? If not, then maybe you will discover what the proper value for δ should be. To check if the current guess of $\delta = \delta'$ is correct, it is necessary to see if the certain property in B2 holds for δ' and also if the something happens. From B2, the certain property is that $\delta > 0$, but since $\delta = \delta'$ and $\delta' > 0$, it must be that $\delta > 0$. Thus, it remains only to verify that, for $\delta = \delta'$:

B3: For all y with $|x - y| < \delta$, $|f(x) - f(y)| < \varepsilon'$.

Looking at B3, you should recognize the quantifier "for all" in the backward process and you should use the choose method to select a particular value of y, say y', with $|x - y'| < \delta$. The choose method then requires you to show that the something happens, in this case:

B4: $|f(x) - f(y')| < \varepsilon'$.

To see if B4 is true, the hypothesis still has some unused information. Specifically, the number $c > 0$ has not been used, nor has the statement:

A1: For all y with $|x - y| < \delta'$, $|f(x) - f(y)| \leq c|x - y|$.

Upon recognizing the quantifier "for all" in the forward process, perhaps you should consider using specialization; the only question is which value of y to specialize to. Why not try the value of y' that was obtained in the backward process? Fortunately, y' was chosen to have the certain property in A1 (i.e., $|x - y'| < \delta$ and $\delta = \delta'$, so $|x - y'| < \delta'$), and therefore, you can specialize A1 to y', obtaining:

A2: $|f(x) - f(y')| \leq c|x - y'|$.

Recall that the last statement obtained in the backward process was B4, so the idea is to see if A2 can be made to look more like B4. For instance, since y' was chosen so that $|x - y'| < \delta$, A2 can be rewritten as:

A3: $|f(x) - f(y')| \leq c\delta$.

B4 would be obtained if $c\delta$ were known to be $< \varepsilon'$. Unfortunately, $\delta = \delta'$, but you do not know that $c\delta' < \varepsilon'$. This means that the original guess of $\delta = \delta'$ was incorrect. Perhaps δ should have been chosen > 0 so that $c\delta < \varepsilon'$, or equivalently, since $c > 0$, why not choose $0 < \delta < \varepsilon'/c$?

In order to see if the new "guess" of $0 < \delta < \varepsilon'/c$ is correct, it is necessary to check if, for this value of δ, the certain property in B2 holds and also whether the something happens. Clearly δ has been chosen to be > 0 and thus has the certain property. It remains only to verify that the something happens, in this case, that B3 is true.

As before, one would proceed with the choose method to select y' with $|x - y'| < \delta$, and again one is led to showing that B4 is true. The previous approach was to specialize A1 to y'. This time, however, there is a problem because y' is not known to satisfy the certain property in A1, i.e., that $|x - y'| < \delta'$. Unfortunately, all you do know is that $|x - y'| < \delta$ and $0 < \delta < \varepsilon'/c$. If only you could apply specialization to A1, then you would obtain precisely A2, and finally, since $c\delta < \varepsilon'$, you could reach the desired conclusion that B4 is true.

Can you figure out how to choose δ so that both $c\delta < \varepsilon'$ and so that A1 can be specialized to y'? The answer is to choose $0 < \delta < \min\{\delta', \varepsilon'/c\}$, for then, when y' is chosen with $|x - y'| < \delta$, it will follow that $|x - y'| < \delta'$ because $\delta < \delta'$. Thus, it will be possible to specialize A1 to y'. Also, from A2 and the fact that $\delta < \varepsilon'/c$, it will be possible to conclude that $|f(x) - f(y')| \leq c|x - y'| < c\delta \leq c(\varepsilon'/c) = \varepsilon'$, thus completing the proof.

Proof of Example 18. To show that f is continuous at x, let $\varepsilon' > 0$. By the hypothesis, it is possible to construct $0 < \delta < \min\{\delta', \varepsilon'/c\}$. Then, for y' with $|x - y'| < \delta$, it follows that $|x - y'| < \delta'$ and so, by the hypothesis, $|f(x) - f(y')| \leq c|x - y'| < c\delta$. Furthermore, since $\delta < \varepsilon'/c$, one has $|f(x) - f(y')| < c\delta \leq c(\varepsilon'/c) = \varepsilon'$, and the proof is complete.//

As with any language, reading, writing, and speaking come only with practice. The proof techniques are designed to get you started in the right direction.

solutions to exercises

Chapter 1

1.1. (a), (c), (e), and (f) are statements.

1.2. (a) Hypothesis: The right triangle XYZ with sides of lengths x and y, and hypotenuse of length z, has an area of $z^2/4$.
Conclusion: The triangle XYZ is isosceles.
(b) Hypothesis: n is an even integer.
Conclusion: n^2 is an even integer.
(c) Hypothesis: a, b, c, d, e, and f are real numbers that satisfy the property that $ad - bc \neq 0$.
Conclusion: The two linear equations $ax + by = e$ and $cx + dy = f$ can be solved for x and y.
(d) Hypothesis: n is a positive integer.
Conclusion: The sum of the first n integers is $n(n + 1)/2$.
(e) Hypothesis: r is a real number and satisfies $r^2 = 2$.
Conclusion: r is an irrational number.
(f) Hypothesis: p and q are positive real numbers with $\sqrt{pq} \neq (p + q)/2$.
Conclusion: $p \neq q$.
(g) Hypothesis: x is a real number.
Conclusion: The minimum value of $x(x - 1)$ is at least $-1/4$.

1.3. If we want to prove that "A => B" is true and we know that B is false, then A should also be false. The reason is that if A is false, then it does not matter whether B is true or false, and Table 1 ensures that "A => B" is true. On the other hand, if A is true and B is false, then "A => B" would be false.

1.4. (a) True, because A is false.
     (b) True, because A and B are both true.
     (c) True, because B is true. The truth of A
         does not matter.
     (d) True if x ≠ 3 because then A is false.
         False if x = 3 because then A is true.

1.5. (a) (T = true, F = false)

A	B	C	(B=>C)	A=>(B=>C)
T	T	T	T	T
T	T	F	F	F
T	F	T	T	T
T	F	F	T	T
F	T	T	T	T
F	T	F	F	T
F	F	T	T	T
F	F	F	T	T

   (b) (T = true, F = false)

A	B	C	(A=>B)	(A=>B)=>C
T	T	T	T	T
T	T	F	T	F
T	F	T	F	T
T	F	F	F	T
F	T	T	T	T
F	T	F	T	F
F	F	T	T	T
F	F	F	T	F

Chapter 2

2.1. The forward process is a process that makes
     specific use of the information contained in
     statement A, the hypothesis. The backward
     process is a process that tries to find a chain

of statements leading directly to the fact that statement B, the conclusion, is true. Incorporated in the backward process is the abstraction process that is directed toward generating this chain of statements, one at a time.

Specifically, the backward process works by beginning with the statement B that we are trying to conclude is true. Then we use the abstraction process to ask and answer the abstraction questions, deriving a sequence of new statements with the property that if the sequence of new statements is true, then B is true. The abstraction process will continue in this manner until either we obtain the statement A, or until we can no longer ask and/or answer the abstraction question. There can be difficulties in the backward process, such as the possibility of more than one abstraction question. If this occurs, then we must use the information in statement A to help us choose the appropriate one. A second difficulty is that there may be more than one answer to the abstraction question and some of these answers may not lead to the completion of the proof.

The forward process begins with the statement A, which is assumed to be true, and derives from it a sequence of new statements that are true as a result of statement A being true. Every new statement derived from A should be directed toward linking up with the last statement derived in the backward process. The last statement of the backward process acts as the guiding light in the forward process, just as the last statement in the forward process helps us to choose the right abstraction question and the right abstraction answer.

2.2. (c) is incorrect because it uses the specific notation given in the problem.

2.3. (a) is correct because it asks, abstractly, how the statement B can be proven true. (b) and (c) are not valid because they use the specific

notation in the problem. Statement (d) is an
incorrect question for this problem.

2.4. (a) How can I show that two lines are parallel?
How can I show that two lines do not
intersect? How can I show that two lines
tangent to a circle are parallel? How can I
show that two tangent lines passing through
the endpoints of the diameter of a circle
are parallel?

(b) How can I show that a function is
continuous? How can I show that the sum of
two functions is continuous? How can I show
that the sum of two continuous functions is
continuous?

(c) How can I show that an integer is even? How
can I show that a number is an even integer?
How can I show that an integer is not odd?
How can I show that an integer squared is
even?

(d) How can I show that the solution to a second
degree polynomial is a specific integer?
How can I solve a quadratic equation? How
can I show that two quadratic equations
share a common root?

2.5. (a) Show that their difference equals zero.
Show that one is $\le$ the other and vice
versa. Show that their ratio is one. Show
that they are both equal to a third number.

(b) Show that corresponding side-angle-sides are
equal. Show that their corresponding
angle-side-angles are equal. Show that
corresponding side-side-sides are equal.
Show that they are both congruent to a third
triangle.

(c) Show that they lie in the same plane and do
not intersect. Show that they are both
perpendicular to a third line. Show that
they have equal slopes. Show that their
corresponding equations are identical or
have no common solution. Show that they are
each parallel to a third line.

(d) Show that it has three 90 degree angles.
Show that it is a square. Show that it is a
parallelogram with one right angle.

2.6. (a) (1) How can I show that the solution to a quadratic equation is positive?
(2) Show that the quadratic formula gives a positive solution.
(3) Show that the solution $-b/a$ is positive.
(b) (1) How can I show that a triangle is equilateral?
(2) Show that three sides have equal length or, show that three angles are equal.
(3) Show that $\overline{RT} = \overline{ST} = \overline{SR}$, or show that angle R = angle S = angle T.

2.7. (a) $(x - 2)(x - 1) < 0$.
$x(x - 3) < - 2$.
$-x^2 + 3x - 2 > 0$.

(b) $x/z = 1/\sqrt{2}$.
Angle X has 45 degrees.
$\cos(X) = 1/\sqrt{2}$.

(c) The circle has its center at $(3, 2)$.
The circle has a radius of 5.
The circle crosses the y axis at $(0, 6)$ and $(0, -2)$.
$x^2 - 6x + 9 + y^2 - 4y + 4 = 25$.

(d) $\overline{UV} = \overline{VW} = \overline{UW}$.
Angle U = angle W = angle V = 60 degrees.
The triangle is isosceles.
The height of the triangle is $\sqrt{3}/2$ times the length of a side.

2.8. (d) is not valid because "$x \neq 5$" is not stated in the hypothesis, and so, if $x = 5$, then it will not be possible to divide by $x - 5$.

2.9. (a) Outline of proof. An abstraction question associated with the conclusion is "How can I show that a real number (namely x) is 0?" To show that $x = 0$, it will be established that both $x \leq 0$ and $x \geq 0$. Working forward from the hypothesis immediately establishes that $x \geq 0$. To see that $x \leq 0$, it will be shown that $x = -y$ and $-y \leq 0$. Both of these statements follow by working forward from the hypothesis that $x + y = 0$ (so $x = -y$)

and $y \geq 0$ (so $-y \leq 0$). It remains only to show that $y = 0$, which follows by working forward from the fact that $x = 0$ and the hypothesis that $x + y = 0$. Specifically, $0 = x + y = 0 + y = y$.

(b) Proof. To see that both $x = 0$ and $y = 0$, it will first be shown that $x \geq 0$ (which is given in the hypothesis) and $x \leq 0$. The latter is accomplished by showing that $x = -y$ and that $-y \leq 0$. To see that $x = -y$, observe that the hypothesis states that $x + y = 0$. Similarly, $-y \leq 0$, because the hypothesis states that $y \geq 0$. Thus, $x = 0$.

Finally, to see that $y = 0$, one can use the fact that $x = 0$ and the hypothesis that $x + y = 0$ to reach the desired conclusion.//

2.10. (a) The number to the left of each line in the diagram below indicates which rule is being used.

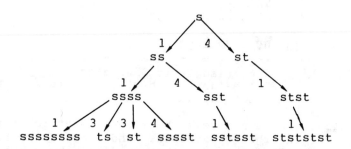

(b) The number to the left of each line in the diagram below indicates which rule is being used.

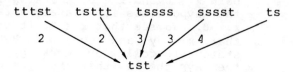

(c)
A :	s	given
A1:	ss	rule 1
A2:	ssss	rule 1
B1:	sssst	rule 4
B :	tst	rule 3

(d)
A :	s	given
A1:	tst	from part c
A2:	tsttst	rule 1
A3:	tsst	rule 2
A4:	tssttsst	rule 1
B1:	tsssst	rule 2
B :	ttst	rule 3

2.11. Outline of proof. In this problem one has:

A: The right triangle XYZ is isosceles.

B: The area of triangle XYZ is $z^2/4$.

An abstraction question for B is "How can I show that the area of a triangle is equal to a particular value?" One answer is to use the formula for computing the area of a triangle to show that

B1: $z^2/4 = xy/2$

Working forward from the hypothesis that triangle XYZ is isosceles, one has:

A1: $x = y$

A2: $x - y = 0$

Since XYZ is a right triangle, from the Pythagorean theorem, we obtain

A3: $z^2 = x^2 + y^2$

From the statement A2, if we square both sides of the equation and perform some algebraic manipulations, we obtain

A4: $(x - y)^2 = 0$

A5: $x^2 - 2xy + y^2 = 0$

A6: $x^2 + y^2 = 2xy$

Substituting A3 into A6 yields

A7: $z^2 = 2xy$

Dividing both sides by 4 finally yields the desired result:

A8: $z^2/4 = xy/2$

Proof. From the hypothesis, one knows that $x = y$, or equivalently, that $x - y = 0$. Performing some algebraic manipulations, one obtains $x^2 + y^2 = 2xy$. By the Pythagorean theorem, $z^2 = x^2 + y^2$ and on substituting z^2 for $x^2 + y^2$, one obtains $z^2 = 2xy$, or equivalently, $z^2/4 = xy/2$. From the formula for the area of a right triangle, the area of XYZ $= xy/2$. Hence $z^2/4$ is the area of the triangle.//

2.12. Outline of proof. An abstraction question associated with the conclusion is "How can I show that a triangle is equilateral?" One answer is to show that all three sides have equal length, specifically, $\overline{RS} = \overline{ST} = \overline{RT}$. To see that $\overline{RS} = \overline{ST}$, one can work forward from the hypothesis to establish that triangle RSU is congruent to triangle SUT. Specifically, by the hypothesis, $\overline{RU} = \overline{UT}$ and, in addition, angle RUS = angle SUT = 90 degrees. Of course $\overline{SU} = \overline{SU}$, so the side-angle-side theorem states that the two triangles are congruent. Finally, to see that $\overline{RS} = \overline{RT}$, work forward from the hypothesis to obtain the conclusion that $\overline{RS} = 2\overline{RU} = \overline{RU} + \overline{UT} = \overline{RT}$.

Proof. To see that triangle RST is equilateral, it will actually be shown that $\overline{RS} = \overline{ST} = \overline{RT}$. To that end, the hypothesis that SU is a perpendicular bisector of RT ensures (by the side-angle-side theorem) that triangle RSU is congruent to triangle SUT. Hence, $\overline{RS} = \overline{ST}$. To see that $\overline{RS} = \overline{RT}$, by the hypothesis, one can easily conclude that $\overline{RS} = 2\overline{RU} = \overline{RU} + \overline{UT} = \overline{RT}$.//

Chapter 3

3.1. (a) Abs.   Qn: How can I show that an integer is
                      odd?
          Abs.   Ans: Show that the integer equals two
                       times some integer plus one.
          Spec.   Ans: Show that $n^2 = 2k + 1$.
      (b)·Abs.   Qn: How can I show that a real number
                      is a rational number?
          Abs.   Ans: Show that the real number is
                       equal to the ratio of two
                       integers, where the integer in
                       the denominator is not equal to
                       zero.
          Spec.   Ans: Show that $s/t = p/q$, where p and
                       q are integers and $q \neq 0$.
      (c) Abs.   Qn: How can I show that two pairs of
                      real numbers are equal?
          Abs.   Ans: Show that the first and second
                       elements of one pair of real
                       numbers are equal to the first
                       and second elements of the other
                       pair, respectively.
          Spec.   Ans: Show that $x_1 = x_2$ and $y_1 = y_2$.
      (d) Abs.   Qn: How can I show that an integer is
                      prime?
          Abs.   Ans: Show that the integer is
                       positive, greater than 1, and can
                       only be divided by itself and
                       one.
          Spec.   Ans: Show that $n > 1$ and, if p is an
                       integer that divides n, then
                       $p = 1$ or $p = n$.
      (e) Abs.   Qn: How can I show that an integer
                      divides another integer?
          Abs.   Ans: Show that the second integer
                       equals the product of the first
                       integer with another integer, and
                       that the first integer is not
                       equal to zero.
          Spec.   Ans: Show that the following
                       expression holds true for some
                       integer k:
                       $(n - 1)^3 + n^3 + (n + 1)^3 = 9k$.

3.2. (A is the hypothesis and A1 is the result of working forward one step).

(a) A : n is an odd integer.
    A1: n = 2k + 1, where k is an integer.

(b) A : s and t are rational numbers with t ≠ 0.
    A1: s = p/q, where p and q are integers with q ≠ 0. Also, t = a/b, where a and b are integers with b ≠ 0.

(c) A : Triangle RST is equilateral.
    A1: $\overline{RS}$ = $\overline{ST}$ = $\overline{RT}$, and angle(R) = angle(S) = angle(T).

(d) A : sin(X) = cos(X).
    A1: x/z = y/z (or, x = y).

(e) A : a, b, c are integers for which a divides b and b divides c.
    A1: b = pa and c = qb, where p and q are two integers and, a ≠ 0, b ≠ 0.

3.3. (T = true, F = false)

(a) Truth table for converse of "A implies B."

A	B	"A Implies B"	"B Implies A"
T	T	T	T
T	F	F	T
F	T	T	F
F	F	T	T

(b) Truth table for inverse of "A implies B."

A	B	NOT A	NOT B	"NOT A Implies NOT B"
T	T	F	F	T
T	F	F	T	T
F	T	T	F	F
F	F	T	T	T

Note: Converse and inverse of "A implies B" are

equivalent. Both are false if and only if
A is false and B is true.

(c) Truth table for "A OR B."

A	B	"A OR B"
T	T	T
T	F	T
F	T	T
F	F	F

(d) Truth table for "A AND B."

A	B	"A AND B"
T	T	T
T	F	F
F	T	F
F	F	F

(e) Truth table for "A AND NOT B"

A	B	NOT B	"A AND NOT B"
T	T	F	F
T	F	T	T
F	T	F	F
F	F	T	F

(f) Truth table for "(NOT A) OR B."

A	NOT A	B	(NOT A) OR B	"A Implies B"
T	F	T	T	T
T	F	F	F	F
F	T	T	T	T
F	T	F	T	T

Note: "A implies B" and "NOT A OR B" are
equivalent. Both are false when A is true
and B is false.

3.4. (a) Converse : if n is an even integer, then n^2 is even.

Inverse : if n is an integer for which n^2 is not even, then n is odd.

Contra-positive : if n is an odd integer, then n^2 is odd.

(b) Converse : if r is not rational, then r is a real number such that $r^2 = 2$.

Inverse : if r is a real number such that $r^2 \neq 2$, then r is rational.

Contra-positive : if r is rational, then r is a real number such that $r^2 \neq 2$.

(c) Converse : if the quadrilateral ABCD is a rectangle, then the quadrilateral ABCD is a parallelogram with one right angle.

Inverse : if the quadrilateral ABCD is not a parallelogram with one right angle, then the quadrilateral ABCD is not a rectangle.

Contra-positive : if the quadrilateral ABCD is not a rectangle, then ABCD is not a parallelogram with one right angle.

(d) Converse : if $t = \pi/4$, then t is an angle for which $\sin(t) = \cos(t)$ and $0 < t < \pi$.

Inverse : if t is an angle for which $\sin(t) \neq \cos(t)$ and $0 < t < \pi$, then $t \neq \pi/4$.

Contra-positive : if $t \neq \pi/4$, then t is an angle for which $0 < t < \pi$, and $\sin(t) \neq \cos(t)$.

3.5. Outline of proof. The forward-backward method gives rise to the abstraction question "How can I show an integer (namely n^2) is odd?" The definition for an odd integer is used to answer the abstraction question which means that we have to show that $n^2 = 2k + 1$ for some integer k. We now turn toward the hypothesis and work forward to reach the desired conclusion.

Since n is an odd integer, by definition, n = 2m + 1 for some integer m. Therefore,

$$n^2 = (2m + 1)^2$$

$$= 4m^2 + 4m + 1$$

$$= 2(2m^2 + 2m) + 1$$

Thus the desired value for k is $(2m^2 + 2m)$, and since m is an integer, $(2m^2 + 2m)$ is an integer. Hence it has been shown that n^2 can be expressed as 2 times some integer plus 1, which completes the proof.

Proof. Since n is an odd integer, there is an integer m for which n = 2m + 1, and therefore,

$$n^2 = (2m + 1)^2$$

$$= 4m^2 + 4m + 1$$

$$= 2(2m^2 + 2m) + 1,$$

and hence n^2 is an odd integer.//

3.6. Outline of proof. Proceeding by the forward-backward method, one is led to the abstraction question "How can I show an integer (namely mn) is odd?" By using the definition of an odd integer, this question can be answered by showing that mn can be expressed as 2 times some integer plus 1. We now turn to the forward process to find out which integer.

Since m is an odd integer and n is an odd integer, one has m = 2b + 1 for some integer b, and n = 2c + 1 for integer c. Therefore,

$$mn = (2b + 1)(2c + 1)$$

$$= 4bc + 2b + 2c + 1$$

$$= 2(b + c + 2bc) + 1.$$

Thus it has been shown that mn can be written as 2 times another integer plus 1, that other integer being (b + c + 2bc), and this completes the proof.

Proof. Since m and n are odd integers, m = 2b + 1 and n = 2c + 1, where b and c are integers. Thus

$$mn = (2b + 1)(2c + 1)$$

$$= 2(b + c + 2bc) + 1.$$

Hence mn is an odd integer.//

3.7. Outline of proof. Using the forward-backward method, one is led to the abstraction question "How can I show that one statement (namely A) implies another statement (namely C)?" According to Table 1, the answer is to assume that the statement to the left of the word "implies" is true, and then reach the conclusion that the statement to the right of the word "implies" is true. In this specific case, we assume A to be true and we try to prove that C is also true.

Working forward from the information given in the hypothesis, we find that since "A implies B" is true and A is true, B must be true. Since B is true, and "B implies C" is true, C must also be true. Hence the proof is complete.

Proof. To conclude that "A implies C" is true, assume that A is true. By the hypothesis, "A implies B" is true, so B must be true. Finally, since "B implies C" is true, it must be that C is true, thus completing the proof.//

3.8. Outline of proof. The forward-backward method gives rise to the abstraction question "How can I show that two statements (namely A and B) are equivalent?" Definition 8 indicates that one must show that "A implies B" is true (which is given in the hypothesis), and "B implies A" is true. The hypothesis that "B implies C" and "C implies A," together with Exercise 3.7, ensures that "B implies A" is true. The proof that A is equivalent to C is similar.

Proof. In order to show that A is equivalent to B, one need only show that "B implies A," since the hypothesis states that "A implies B." The fact that "B implies A" follows from the hypothesis that "B implies C" and "C implies A," together with Exercise 3.7. The proof that A is equivalent to C is omitted.//

3.9. (a) We will require six proofs to show that A is equivalent to each of the three alternatives. The six proofs are: A => B, B => A, A => C, C => A, A => D, and D => A.

(b) We would require only four proofs, namely, A => B, B => C, C => D, and D => A.

(c) If the four statements in part (b) above are true, then you can show that A is equivalent to any of the alternatives by using Exercise 3.7. For instance, to show that A is equivalent to D, one already knows that "D implies A." Also, by Exercise 3.7, since "A implies B," "B implies C," and "C implies D," it follows that "A implies D."

3.10. (a) Outline of proof. The forward-backward method gives rise to the abstraction question "How can I show that a triangle is isosceles?" Using the definition of an isosceles triangle, we have to show that two of its sides are equal, which in this specific case means that we have to show that $u = v$. Working forward from the hypothesis, we know that $\sin(U) = \sqrt{u/2v}$. By the definition of sine, $\sin(U) = u/w$, so $\sqrt{u/2v} = u/w$, and by applying algebraic manipulations, one obtains that $w^2 = 2uv$. Furthermore, by the Pythagorean theorem, $u^2 + v^2 = w^2$. On substituting for w^2, one has $u^2 + v^2 = 2uv$, and consequently, $u^2 - 2uv + v^2 = 0$. On factoring, and then taking the square root of both sides of the equation, it follows that $u - v = 0$, or, $u = v$, completing the proof.

Proof. Since $\sin(U) = \sqrt{u/2v}$ and also $\sin(U) = u/w$, $\sqrt{u/2v} = u/w$, or, $w^2 = 2uv$. Now, by Pythagorean theorem, $w^2 = u^2 + v^2$, and on substituting $2uv$ for w^2, and then performing some algebraic manipulations, one obtains $u = v.//$

(b) Outline of proof. In order to verify the hypothesis of Example 1 for the current triangle UVW, it is necessary to match up the notation. Specifically, $x = u$, $y = v$, and $z = w$. Then it must be shown that $uv/2 = w^2/4$. Working forward <u>from</u> the current hypothesis that $\sin(U) = \sqrt{u/2v}$, and since $\sin(U) = u/w$, one has $\sqrt{u/2v} = u/w$, or, $u/2v = u^2/w^2$, or, $w^2 = 2uv$, and finally that $uv/2 = w^2/4$. Observe also that triangle UVW is a right triangle.

Proof. By the hypothesis, $\sin(U) = \sqrt{u/2v}$, and from the definition of sine, $\sin(U) = u/w$, thus $\sqrt{u/2v} = u/w$. By applying algebraic manipulations, one obtains $uv/2 = w^2/4$. Hence, the hypothesis of Example 1 holds for the current right triangle UVW, and consequently the triangle is isosceles.$//$

(c) Outline of proof. In order to verify the hypothesis of Example 3 for the current triangle UVW, it is necessary to match up the notation. Specifically, $r = u$, $s = v$, and $t = w$. Thus it must be shown that $w = \sqrt{2uv}$ but, as in the proof of part (b), $\sqrt{u/2v} = u/w$, so $u/2v = u^2/w^2$, or, $w^2 = 2uv$, or, $w = \sqrt{2uv}$. Observe also that triangle UVW is a right triangle.

Proof. By the hypothesis, $\sin(U) = \sqrt{u/2v}$, and from the definition of sine, $\sin(U) = u/w$, thus one has $\sqrt{u/2v} = u/w$. By algebraic manipulations, one obtains $w = \sqrt{2uv}$. Hence the hypothesis of Example 3 holds for the current right triangle UVW, and consequently the triangle must be isosceles.$//$

Chapter 4

4.1.

	Object	Certain property	Something happens
(a)	mountain in Himalyas	over 20,000 feet	taller than every other mountain in the world
(b)	integer x	none	$x^2 - 5x/2 + 3/2 = 0$
(c)	line ℓ'	through P not on ℓ	ℓ' parallel to ℓ
(d)	angle t	$0 < t < \pi/2$	$\sin(t) = \cos(t)$
(e)	rational numbers r,s	between x and y	$|r - s| < 0.001$

4.2. (a) A triangle XYZ is isosceles if $\exists$ two sides $\ni$ their lengths are equal.
(b) Given an angle t, $\exists$ an angle t' $\ni$ tangent of t' is greater than tangent of t.
(c) At a party of n people, $\exists$ at least two people $\ni$ they have the same number of friends.
(d) For a polynomial of degree n, say P(x), $\exists$ exactly n complex roots, $r_1, \ldots, r_n \ni$ $P(r_1) = \ldots = P(r_n) = 0$.

4.3. Outline of proof. Using the construction method, we will find values of x such that $x^2 - 5x/2 + 3/2 = 0$. From the quadratic formula, the values of x are:

$$(5/2 \pm \sqrt{25/4 - 12/2})/2 = (5/2 \pm 1/2)/2,$$

or, x equals 1 or 3/2. Now if we substitute these values of x into $x^2 - 5x/2 + 3/2 = 0$, we see that the quadratic equation is satisfied.
(a) Proof. Using the quadratic formula for $x^2 - 5x/2 + 3/2 = 0$, we find that x = 1 or

$x = 3/2$. Thus, there exists an integer, namely $x = 1$, such that $x^2 - 5x/2 + 3/2 = 0$. The integer is unique.//

(b) Proof. Using the quadratic formula on $x^2 - 5x/2 + 3/2 = 0$, we find that $x = 1$ or $x = 3/2$. Thus there exists a real number for x such that $x^2 - 5x/2 + 3/2 = 0$. The real number x is not unique.//

4.4. Outline of proof. The forward-backward method gives rise to the abstraction question "How can I show that an integer (namely a) divides another integer (namely c)?" By Definition 1, one answer is to show that there is an integer k such that $c = ak$. The appearance of the quantifier "there is" suggests turning to the forward process to construct the desired k.

From the hypothesis that $a|b$ and $b|c$, and by Definition 1, there are integers p and q such that $b = ap$ and $c = bq$. Therefore, it follows that $c = bq = (ap)q = a(pq)$, and the desired integer k is $k = pq$.

Proof. Since $a|b$ and $b|c$, by definition, there are integers p and q for which $b = ap$ and $c = bq$. But then $c = bq = (ap)q = a(pq)$. Thus, $a|c$.//

4.5. Outline of proof. The forward-backward method gives rise to the abstraction question "How can I show that a real number (namely s/t) is rational?" By Definition 11, one answer is to show that there are integers p and q with $q \neq 0$ such that $s/t = p/q$. The appearance of the quantifier "there are" suggests turning to the forward process to construct the desired p and q.

From the hypothesis that s and t are rational numbers, and by Definition 11, there are integers a, b, c, and d with $b \neq 0$ and $d \neq 0$ such that $s = a/b$ and $t = c/d$. Furthermore, since $t \neq 0$, $c \neq 0$, and thus $bc \neq 0$. Hence $s/t = (a/b)/(c/d) = ad/bc$. So the desired integers p and q are $p = ad$ and

q = bc. Observe that since b ≠ 0 and c ≠ 0,
q ≠ 0, and furthermore, s/t = p/q.

Proof. Since s and t are rational, by
definition, there are integers a, b, c, and d
with b ≠ 0 and d ≠ 0 such that s = a/b and
t = c/d. Furthermore, since t ≠ 0, c ≠ 0.
Constructing p = ad and q = bc, and noting that
q ≠ 0, one has s/t = (a/b)/(c/d) = ad/bc = p/q,
and hence s/t is rational.//

Chapter 5

5.1. (a) Object: real number x
         Certain property: none
         Something happens: $f(x) \leq f(x^*)$

     (b) Object: element x
         Certain property: x in S
         Something happens: $g(x) \geq f(x)$

     (c) Object: element x
         Certain property: x in S
         Something happens: $x \leq u$

     (d) Object: real number ε
         Certain property: ε > 0
         Something happens: there is x in S such that
         $x > u - \varepsilon$

     (e) Object: elements x and y, and real numbers t
         Certain property: x and y in C, and
         $0 \leq t \leq 1$
         Something happens: $tx + (1 - t)y$ is an
         element of C

     (f) Object: real numbers x, y, and t
         Certain property: $0 \leq t \leq 1$
         Something happens:
         $f(tx + (1 - t)y) \leq tf(x) + (1 - t)f(y)$

(g) Object: real number ε
Certain property: $\varepsilon > 0$
Something happens: there is a real number $\delta > 0$ such that, for all real numbers y with $|x - y| < \delta$, $|f(x) - f(y)| < \varepsilon$

(h) Object: real number ε
Certain property: $\varepsilon > 0$
Something happens: there is an integer k' such that for all integers $k > k'$, $|x^k - x| < \varepsilon$

5.2. (a) Let x' be a real number. It will be shown that $f(x') \leq f(x^*)$.

(b) Let x' be an element in S. It will be shown that $g(x') \geq f(x')$.

(c) Let x' be an element in S. It will be shown that $x' \leq u$.

(d) Let ε' be a real number such that $\varepsilon' > 0$. It will be shown that there is an x in S such that $x > u - \varepsilon'$.

(e) Let x', y' be elements in C, and let t' be a real number between 0 and 1. It will be shown that $t'x' + (1 - t')y'$ is an element of C.

(f) Let x', y', t' be real numbers such that $0 \leq t' \leq 1$. It will be shown that $f(t'x' + (1-t')y') \leq t'f(x') + (1-t')f(y')$.

(g) Let ε' be a real number such that $\varepsilon' > 0$. It will be shown that there is a real number $\delta > 0$ such that, for all real numbers y with $|x - y| < \delta$, $|f(x) - f(y)| < \varepsilon'$.

(h) Let ε' be a real number such that $\varepsilon' > 0$. It will be shown that there is an integer k' such that, for all integers $k > k'$, $|x^k - x| < \varepsilon'$.

5.3. When using the choose method to show that "for all objects with a certain property, something happens," you would choose one particular object that does have the certain property. You would then work forward from the certain property to reach the conclusion that the something happens. This is precisely the same as using the forward-backward method to show that "if x is an object with certain property, then the something happens," whereby you would work forward from the fact that x is an object with the certain property, and backward from the something that happens. In other words, a statement containing the quantifier "for all" can be converted into an equivalent statement having the form "if . . . then . . . ."

5.4. (a) ∃ a mountain ∋ ∀ other mountains, this one is taller than the others.
   (b) ∀ angle t, sin(2t) = 2sin(t)cos(t).
   (c) ∀ two nonnegative real numbers p and q, $\sqrt{pq} \leq (p + q)/2$.
   (d) ∀ two real numbers x and y with x < y, ∃ a rational number r ∋ x < r < y.

5.5. (a) First you would use the construction method to construct M > 0, and then use the choose method to choose x' in S for which it must be shown that |x'| ≤ M.
   (b) First you would use the choose method and choose M' > 0, and then use the construction method to construct an x in S for which |x| > M'.
   (c) First you would use the choose method to choose ε' > 0, then use the construction method to construct δ > 0, and then again use the choose method to choose x' and y' with |x' - y'| < δ, for which it must be shown that |f(x') - f(y')| < ε'.

5.6. Outline of proof. The forward-backward method gives rise to the abstraction question "How can I show that a set (namely T) is a subset of another set (namely S)?" The definition provides the answer that one must show that

   B1: for all t in T, t is in S.

The appearance of the quantifier "for all" in the backward process suggests using the choose method to choose an element t' in T for which it must be shown that

   B2: t' is in S.

This, in turn, is done by showing that t'
satisfies the defining property of S, i.e., that

B3: $(t')^2 - 3t' + 2 \leq 0$.

Working forward from the fact that t' is in
T, i.e., that it satisfies the defining property
of T, one knows that

A1: $1 \leq t' \leq 2$.

Consequently, $(t' - 1) \geq 0$ and $(t' - 2) \leq 0$, so
$(t')^2 - 3t' + 2 = (t' - 1)(t' - 2) \leq 0$,   thus
establishing B3 and completing the proof.

Proof. To show that $T \subseteq S$, let t' be an element
of T. It will be shown that t' is in S. Since
t' is in T, $1 \leq t' \leq 2$, so $(t' - 1) \geq 0$ and
$(t' - 2) \leq 0$. Thus,

$(t')^2 - 3t' + 2 = (t' - 1)(t' - 2) \leq 0$

and so t' is in S.//

5.7. Outline of proof. The key word "for every" in
the conclusion suggests using the choose method.
To that end, let x' > 2 be a real number. To
construct the desired y < 0, we want

$x' = 2y/(1 + y)$

or

$x' + x'y = 2y$

or

$x' = 2y - x'y = y(2 - x')$

or

$y = x'/(2 - x')$.

Hence the desired y is $x'/(2 - x')$, and it is
easily shown that, for this value of y,
$x' = 2y/(1 + y)$. However, it must also be shown
that y < 0, which it is, since x' > 2.

Proof. Let x' > 2, and therefore we can
construct $y = x'/(2 - x')$. Since x' > 2, y < 0,
and it is also easy to verify that
$x' = 2y/(1 + y)$.//

5.8. Outline of proof. The forward-backward method
gives rise to the abstraction question "How can
I show a function is convex?" Using the
definition in Exercise 5.1 (f), one must show
that

B1: For all real numbers x and y, and for all t
with $0 \leq t \leq 1$,
$f(tx + (1 - t)y) \leq tf(x) + (1 - t)f(y)$.

The appearance of the quantifier "for all,"
suggests using the choose method. Therefore, we
choose real numbers x' and y', and a real number
t' that satisfies $0 \leq t' \leq 1$. We must show that

$f(t'x' + (1 - t')y') \leq t'f(x') + (1 - t')f(y')$.

But by the hypothesis,

$f(t'x' + (1 - t')y') = m(t'x' + (1 - t')y') + b$

$= mt'x' + my' - mt'y' + b$

$= mt'x' + bt' + my' - mt'y' + b - bt'$

$= t'(mx' + b) + (1 - t') (my' + b)$

$= t'f(x') + (1 - t')f(y')$.

Thus the desired inequality holds.

Proof. To show that f is convex, we must show
that for all real numbers x and y, and for all t
satisfying $0 \leq t \leq 1$,

$f(tx + (1 - t)y) \leq tf(x) + (1 - t)f(y)$.

Let x' and y' be real numbers, and let t'
satisfy $0 \leq t' \leq 1$, then

$f(t'x' + (1 - t')y') = m(t'x' + (1 - t')y') + b$

$= mt'x' + my' - mt'y' + b$

$= t'(mx' + b) + (1 - t') (my' + b)$

$$= t'f(x') + (1 - t')f(y').$$

Thus the inequality holds.//

Chapter 6

6.1. (a) Applicable.
   (b) Not applicable because the statement contains the quantifier "there is" instead of "for all."
   (c) Applicable.
   (d) Applicable.
   (e) Not applicable because in this statement, n is a real number, and induction is applicable only to integers.

6.2. (a) The choose method is used when the following form appears in statement B: "for every object with a certain property, something happens." Induction is used whenever the object is an integer and the certain property is that of being greater than some initial integer. Induction is used in such cases because it is often easier to show that the something happens for n + 1 given that it happens for n, rather than to show that it happens for n, given the certain property, as would be done with the choose method.
   (b) It is not possible to use induction when the object is not an integer because showing that P(n) implies P(n + 1) may "skip over" many values of the object. As a result, the statement will not have been proved for such values.

6.3. Proof. First we show that P(n) is true for n = 1. Replacing n by 1, we must show that 1(1!) = (1 + 1)! - 1. But this is clear since 1(1!) = 1 = (1 + 1)! - 1.

Now we assume that P(n) is true and use that fact to show that P(n + 1) is true. So

P(n)   : 1(1!) + . . . + n(n!) = (n + 1)! - 1

P(n + 1) : 1(1!) + . . . + (n + 1)(n + 1)! =
               (n + 2)! - 1

Starting with the left side of P(n + 1), and then by using P(n), one has

1(1!) + . . . + n(n!) + (n + 1)(n + 1)!

= [1(1!) + . . . + n(n!)] + (n + 1)(n + 1)!

= [(n + 1)! - 1] + (n + 1)(n + 1)!

= (n + 1)![1 + (n + 1)] - 1

= (n + 1)! (n + 2) - 1

= (n + 2)! - 1.

Thus P(n + 1) is true, completing the proof.//

6.4. Proof. First we show that P(n) is true for n = 5. But $2^5 = 32$ and $5^2 = 25$, so $2^5 > 5^2$. Hence we see that it is true for n = 5. Assuming that P(n) is true, we then have to prove that P(n + 1) is true. So

P(n)   : $2^n > n^2$

P(n + 1) : $2^{n+1} > (n + 1)^2$

Starting with the left side of P(n + 1), and using the fact that P(n) is true, one has:

$2^{n+1} = 2(2^n) > 2(n^2)$

To obtain P(n + 1), it must be shown that for n > 5, $2n^2 > (n + 1)^2 = n^2 + 2n + 1$, or, by subtracting n from both sides, that $n^2 > 2n + 1$. This last statement is true for n = 5 (but not for n = 1 or 2), and it can be shown to be true for n > 5 by induction.//

6.5. Proof. The statement is true for a set consisting of one element, say x, because its subsets are {x} and $\emptyset$, i.e., there are $2^1 = 2$ subsets. Assume that for a set with n elements, the number of subsets is 2^n. We will show that for a set with (n + 1) elements, the number of subsets is 2^{n+1}. For a set S with (n + 1) elements we can construct the subsets by listing all of the subsets that are possible using the first n elements, and then, to each such subset, we can add the last element of S. By the induction hypothesis, there are 2^n subsets using n elements, and an additional 2^n subsets are created by adding the last element of S to each of the subsets of n elements. Thus, the total number of subsets of S is $2^n + 2^n = 2^{n+1}$, and the statement has been established for (n + 1).//

6.6. Proof. Let

$$S = 1 + \quad 2 \quad + \ldots + n$$

Then

$$S = n + (n - 1) + \ldots + 1$$

and on adding the two equations one obtains

$$2S = n(n + 1)$$

i.e., $S = n(n + 1)/2$.//

6.7. Proof. Checking for n = 1, we find that $n^3 - n = 1 - 1 = 0$, and six divides 0 since $0 = (6)(0)$. Assuming that the statement is true for (n - 1), we know that 6 divides $(n - 1)^3 - (n - 1)$, or, $(n - 1)^3 - (n - 1) = 6k$ for some integer k. We have to show that $n^3 - n = 6m$ for some integer m. To relate P(n) to P(n + 1) we have

$$(n - 1)^3 - (n - 1) = n^3 - 3n^2 + 3n - 1 - n + 1$$

$$= n^3 - 3n^2 + 2n$$

$$= n^3 - n - (3n^2 - 3n)$$

So $n^3 - n = [(n - 1)^3 - (n - 1)] + 3n^2 - 3n$. By the induction hypothesis, $[(n - 1)^3 - (n - 1)]$ can be divided by 6, so we have to show that $3n^2 - 3n$ can also be divided by 6, or equivalently, that $n^2 - n$ can be divided by 2. However, since $n^2 - n = n(n - 1) =$ the product of two consecutive integers, either n or $(n - 1)$ must be even, and so indeed, $n(n - 1)$ can be divided by 2. Consequently, it follows that $3n^2 - 3n = 6p$ for some integer p. Thus, the desired value for the integer m is $k + p$, for then

$$n^3 - n = [(n - 1)^3 - (n - 1)] + 3(n^2 - n)$$

$$= 6k + 6p$$

$$= 6(k + p)./\!/$$

6.8. (a) Verify that the statement is true for the initial value. Then, assuming that the statement is true for n, prove that it is true for $n - 1$.
   (b) Verify that the statement is true for some integer. Assuming that the statement is true for n, prove that it is true for $n + 1$, and that it is also true for $n - 1$.
   (c) Verify that the statement is true for $n = 1$. Assuming that the statement is true for $2n + 1$, prove that it is also true for $2n + 3$.

6.9. The mistake occurs in the very last sentence where it states that "Then, since all of the colored horses in this (second) group are brown, the uncolored horse must also be brown." How do you know that there is a colored horse in the second group? In fact, when the original group of $(n + 1)$ horses consists of exactly 2 horses, the second group of n horses will not contain a colored horse! The entire difficulty is caused by the fact that the statement should have been verified for the initial integer $n = 2$, not $n = 1$! This, of course, you will be unable to do./\!/

Chapter 7

7.1. Use the choose method when the quantifier "for all" appears in the backward process. Use specialization when the quantifier "for all" appears in the forward process. In other words, use the choose method when you want to show that "for all objects with a certain property, something happens." Use specialization when you know that "for all objects with a certain property, something happens."

7.2. (a) m must be an integer ≥ 5, and if it is, then $2^m > m^2$.

(b) y must be an element of S with $|y| < 5$, and if it is, then y is an element of the set T.

(c) ε' must be > 0, and if it is, then $\exists\ \delta > 0 \ni \forall\ y$ with $|x - y| < \delta$, $|f(x) - f(y)| < \varepsilon'$.

(d) The quadrilateral QRST must have its area equal to the square of the length of a diagonal, and if it does, then QRST is a square.

(e) Angle S of triangle RST must be strictly between 0 and $\pi/4$, and if it is, then $\cos(S) > \sin(S)$.

7.3. Outline of proof. The forward-backward method gives rise to the abstraction question "How can I show that a set (namely R) is a subset of another set (namely T)?" One answer is by the definition, so we show that

B1: for all r in R, r is in T

The appearance of the quantifier "for all" in the backward process indicates that the choose method should be used. So choose an r' in R and, using that information and the hypothesis, it must be shown that r' is in T.

    Turning to the forward process, the hypothesis says that R is a subset of S and S is a subset of T which, by definition, means, respectively, that

A1: for all r in R, r is in S, and

A2: for all s in S, s is in T.

Specializing A1 to r' (which is in R), one has
that r' is in S. Specializing A2 to r' (which
is in S), one has that r' is in T, which is B1,
thus completing the proof.

Proof. To show that R is a subset of T, we must
show that for all r in R, r is in T. Let r' be
in R. By hypothesis, R is a subset of S, so r'
is in S. Also, by hypothesis, S is a subset of
T, so r' is in T.//

7.4. Outline of proof. The forward-backward method
gives rise to the abstraction question "How can
I show that a set (namely S intersect T) is
convex?" One answer is by the definition,
whereby it must be shown that

B1: for all x and y in S intersect T, and for
all 0 ≤ t ≤ 1,   tx + (1 - t)y is in S
intersect T.

The appearance of the quantifier "for all" in
the backward process suggests using the choose
method to choose x' and y' in S intersect T, and
a t' with 0 ≤ t' ≤ 1, for which it must be shown
that

B2: t'x' + (1 - t')y' is in S intersect T.

By working forward from the hypothesis and the
above information, B2 will be established by
showing that t'x' + (1 - t')y' is in both S and
T. Specifically, from the hypothesis that S is
convex, and by the definition, it follows that

A1: for all x and y in S, and for all 0 ≤ t ≤ 1,
tx + (1 - t)y is in S.

Specializing this statement to x', y', and t'
yields that t'x' + (1 - t')y' is in S.   A
similar argument shows that t'x' + (1 - t')y' is
also in T, thus completing the proof.

Proof. To see that S intersect T is convex, let x' and y' be in S intersect T, and let $0 \le t' \le 1$. It will be established that $t'x' + (1 - t')y'$ is in S intersect T. From the hypothesis that S is convex, it follows that $t'x' + (1 - t')y'$ is in S. In a similar manner, $t'x' + (1 - t')y'$ is in T. Thus, one has that $t'x' + (1 - t')y'$ is in S intersect T, and so S intersect T is convex.//

7.5. Outline of proof. The appearance of the quantifier "for all" in the conclusion indicates that the choose method should be used to choose a real number $s' \ge 0$ for which it must be shown that the function $s'f$ is convex. An associated abstraction question is "How can I show that a function (namely $s'f$) is convex?" Using the definition in Exercise 5.1(f), one answer is to show that

B1: for all real numbers x and y, and for all $0 \le t \le 1$,
$s'f(tx + (1 - t)y) \le ts'f(x) + (1 - t)s'f(y)$.

The appearance of the quantifier "for all" in the backward process suggests using the choose method to choose real numbers x' and y', and $0 \le t' \le 1$ for which it must be shown that

B2: $s'f(t'x' + (1 - t')y') \le$
$t's'f(x') + (1 - t')s'f(y')$.

The desired result is obtained by working forward from the hypothesis that f is a convex function. By the definition in Exercise 5.1(f), one knows that

A1: for all real numbers x and y, and for all $0 \le t \le 1$,
$f(tx + (1 - t)y) \le tf(x) + (1 - t)f(y)$.

Specializing this statement to x', y', and t' (noting that $0 \le t' \le 1$) yields

A2: $f(t'x' + (1 - t')y') \le$
$t'f(x') + (1 - t')f(y')$.

The desired statement B2 can be obtained by multiplying both sides of the inequality in A2 by the nonnegative number s', thus completing the proof.

Proof. To show that s'f is convex, let x' and y' be real numbers, and let $0 \leq t' \leq 1$. It will be shown that $s'f(t'x' + (1 - t')y') \leq t's'f(x') + (1 - t')s'f(y')$.

Since f is a convex function by hypothesis, it then follows from the definition that $f(t'x' + (1 - t')y') \leq t'f(x') + (1 - t')f(y')$. The desired result is obtained by multiplying both sides of this inequality by the nonnegative number s'.//

7.6. **Outline of proof.** The forward-backward method gives rise to the abstraction question "How can I show that a set (namely C) is convex?" Using the definition in Exercise 5.1(e), one answer is to show that

B1: for all x and z in the set C, and for all $0 \leq t \leq 1$, tx + (1 - t)z is in C.

The appearance of the quantifier "for all" in the backward process suggests using the choose method to choose x' and z' in C, and a $0 \leq t' \leq 1$. Using this information and the hypothesis, it must be shown that

B2: $t'x' + (1 - t')z'$ is in C.

This, in turn, is done by showing that the point $t'x' + (1 - t')z'$ satisfies the defining property of C, i.e.,

B3: $f(t'x' + (1 - t')z') \leq y$

Turning to the forward process, by hypothesis, f is a convex function. So by the definition in Exercise 5.1(f), it must be that

A1: for all x and z, and for all $0 \leq t \leq 1$, $f(tx + (1 - t)z) \leq tf(x) + (1 - t)f(z)$.

Recognizing the quantifier "for all" in the forward process, specialization will be used. Specifically, Al can be specialized to x', z', and t' (noting that $0 \le t' \le 1$), so

A2: $f(t'x' + (1 - t')z') \le$
    $t'f(x') + (1 - t')f(z')$

Finally, to obtain B2, we will use the fact that x' and z' are in the set C, i.e., they satisfy the defining property of C, thus, $f(x') \le y$ and $f(z') \le y$. So, from A2,

$f(t'x' + (1 - t')z') \le t'f(x') + (1 - t')f(z')$

$$\le t'y + (1 - t')y$$

$$= y,$$

and hence B2 is true, completing the proof.

Proof: To show that C is convex, let x' and z' be elements of C, and let t' satisfy $0 \le t' \le 1$. Hence $f(x') \le y$ and $f(z') \le y$. By the hypothesis, f is a convex function and so

$f(t'x'+ (1 - t')z') \le t'f(x') + (1 - t')f(z')$

$$\le t'y + (1 - t')y$$

$$= y$$

and consequently, $t'x' + (1 - t')z'$ is in C.//

7.7. Outline of proof. The forward-backward method gives rise to the abstraction question "How can I show that a number (namely 1) is a least upper bound for a set (namely S)?" Using the definition in Exercise 5.1(d), one answer is to show that

B1: 1 is an upper bound for S, and, for all $\varepsilon > 0$, there is an x in S such that $x > 1 - \varepsilon$.

To show that the first part of B1 is true, one

is led to the abstraction question "How can I show that a number (namely 1) is an upper bound for a set (namely S)?" Again, the definition in Exercise 5.1(c) can be used to provide the answer that one must show that

B2: for all x in S, x ≤ 1.

Recognizing the quantifier "for all" in the backward process, the choose method is used to choose an element x in S for which it must be shown that

B3: x ≤ 1.

To establish B3, we now make use of the fact that x is in S. To do so, it is important to observe that the set S can be written as

S = {real numbers x: there is an integer n ≥ 2 with x = 1 - 1/n}.

Since x is in S, there is an integer n ≥ 2 for which x = 1 - 1/n, and since n ≥ 2, x = 1 - 1/n ≤ 1, thus B3 is true.

Returning to B1, one must still show that

B4: for all ε > 0, there is an x in S such that x > 1 - ε.

Again, the choose method is used to select an ε > 0 for which it must be shown that

B5: there is an x in S such that x > 1 - ε.

Turning to the forward process, the desired x in S will be constructed by finding an integer n ≥ 2 for which 1 - 1/n > 1 - ε, for then one can construct x = 1 - 1/n. The desired n is any integer > 1/ε, for then 1 - 1/n > 1 - ε, thus completing the proof.

Proof. To see that 1 is an upper bound for S, let x be in S. Hence, there is an integer n ≥ 2 such that x = 1 - 1/n. So x ≤ 1, and therefore 1

is an upper bound for S. To complete the proof,
let $\varepsilon > 0$. An element x in S will be produced
for which $x > 1 - \varepsilon$. Specifically, let $n > 1/\varepsilon$.
Then $x = 1 - 1/n$ satisfies $x > 1 - \varepsilon$.//

Chapter 8

8.1. (a) Assume: ℓ, m, and n are three consecutive
         integers, and that 24 divides
         $\ell^2 + m^2 + n^2 + 1$.
    (b) Assume: Matrix M is not singular, and the
         rows of M are linearly dependent.
    (c) Assume f and g are two functions such that
         $g \geq f$, f is unbounded above, and g is
         bounded above.

8.2. (a) The number of primes is not finite.
    (b) The set of real numbers is not bounded.
    (c) The positive integer p cannot be divided by
         any positive integer other than 1 and p.
    (d) The lines ℓ and ℓ' do not intersect.
    (e) The real number x is not ≥ 5.

8.3. Outline of proof. To use the contradiction
method, we start with the assumptions

   A: n is an integer for which n^2 is even.

   NOT B: n is not even, i.e., n is odd.

We work forward from these assumptions using the
definition of an odd integer to reach the
contradiction that n^2 is odd. Thus, there
exists an integer k such that $n = 2k + 1$. Then

$$n^2 = (2k + 1)^2$$

$$= 4k^2 + 4k + 1$$

$$= 2(2k^2 + 2k) + 1$$

which is of the form $n^2 = 2p + 1$, where $p = 2k^2 + 2k$. Thus n^2 is odd, and this contradiction establishes the result.

Proof. Assume, to the contrary, that n is odd and n^2 is even. Hence, there is an integer k such that, $n = 2k + 1$. Consequently,

$$n^2 = (2k + 1)^2$$

$$= 4k^2 + 4k + 1$$

$$= 2(2k^2 + 2k) + 1.$$

and hence n^2 is odd, contradicting the initial assumption.//

8.4. Outline of Proof. We proceed by assuming that there is a chord of a circle that is longer than its diameter. Starting with this assumption, and using the properties of a circle, we should arrive at a contradiction in order to provide a valid proof.

Let AC be the chord of the circle that is longer than the diameter of the circle. Let AB be a diameter of the circle. This construction is valid since, by definition, a diameter is a line passing through the center terminating at the perimeter of the circle.

Now it follows that angle ACB has 90 degrees (since it is an angle in a semi-circle). Hence the triangle ABC is a right triangle in which AB is the hypotenuse. Then the desired contradiction is that the hypotenuse of a right triangle is shorter than one side of the triangle, which is impossible.

Proof. Assume that there does exist a chord, say AC, of a circle that is longer than a diameter. We construct a diameter that has one of its ends coinciding with one end of the chord. If we join the other ends, then we obtain a right triangle in which the diameter AB is the hypotenuse. Hence $\overline{AB} > \overline{AC}$, which contradicts the initial assumption.//

8.5. Outline of proof. To use the contradiction method, we assume that the two lines ℓ_1 and ℓ_2, which are both perpendicular to a third line ℓ in the plane, are not parallel. Working forward, we can conclude that they do intersect at some point in the plane. Hence the three lines ℓ_1, ℓ_2 and ℓ will form a triangle.

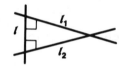

The sum of the three angles of a triangle is 180 degrees. Since two of the angles are 90 degrees, it must be that the third angle of the triangle has zero degrees, an obvious contradiction.

Proof. Assume that ℓ_1 and ℓ_2 are not parallel, and that they are both perpendicular to the same line ℓ. Hence ℓ_1 and ℓ_2 must intersect, and form a triangle in which two of the angles are 90 degrees. Since the sum of the three angles of a triangle is 180 degrees, we are forced to the conclusion that the third angle has zero degrees, a contradiction.//

8.6. Outline of proof. To use contradiction, we proceed by assuming that no two people have the same number of friends, i.e., everybody has a different number of friends. Since there are n

people, each of whom has a different number of
friends, we can list the number of friends each
person has according to an increasing sequence.
In other words,

        person number 1 has   no friends
        person number 2 has   1   friend
        person number 3 has   2   friends
        . . .
        person number n has n - 1 friends.

By doing so, we arrive at the contradiction that
the last person will be friends with all the
other (n - 1) people, including the first one,
who has no friend!

Proof. Assume, to the contrary, that no two
people have the same number of friends. The
people at the party can be numbered in such a
way that

        person 1 has   0   friends
        person 2 has   1   friend
        . . .
        person n has n - 1 friends.

It then follows that the person with (n - 1)
friends is a friend of the person who has no
friends, a contradiction.//

8.7. Outline of proof. By the contradiction method,
it can be assumed that there do exist three
consecutive numbers (n - 1), n, and (n + 1) such
that the cube of the largest is equal to the sum
of the cubes of the remaining two. Now, we can
arrive at a contradiction by showing that no
integer satisfies this equation. Specifically,
we have that

$$(n - 1)^3 + n^3 = (n + 1)^3$$

or
$$n^3 - 3n^2 + 3n - 1 + n^3 = n^3 + 3n^2 + 3n + 1$$

or
$$n^3 - 6n^2 - 2 = 0$$

or
$$n^2(n - 6) = 2$$

Now for $n \leq 6$, $n^2(n - 6) \leq 0$, while for $n > 6$, $n^2(n - 6) > 2$. Hence there is no integer n for which $n^2(n - 6) = 2$.

Proof. Assume that $(n - 1)$, n, and $(n + 1)$ are three consecutive integers such that

$$(n - 1)^3 + n^3 = (n + 1)^3.$$

Then,

$$n^3 - 3n^2 + 3n - 1 + n^3 = n^3 + 3n^2 + 3n + 1$$

or

$$n^3 - 6n^2 = 2$$

or

$$n^2(n - 6) = 2.$$

For $n \leq 6$, $n^2(n - 6) \leq 0$, while for $n > 6$, $n^2(n - 6) > 2$. Hence, there is no integer n for which $n^2(n - 6) = 2.//$

8.8. Outline of proof. By the contradiction method, it can be assumed that the number of primes is finite. If so, then there will be a prime number that is larger than all the other prime numbers. Let n be such a number. Consider the number $n! + 1$, and let p be any prime number that divides $n! + 1$. A contradiction will be reached by showing that $p \leq n$ and $p > n$.

Since n is the largest prime, $p \leq n$. We use the fact that p divides $n! + 1$ to show that $p \neq 1$, $p \neq 2$, . . . , $p \neq n$, and hence it must be that $p > n$. When $n! + 1$ is divided by 2, there is a remainder of 1 since,

$$n! + 1 = [n(n-1) . . . (2)(1)] + 1$$

Similarly, when $n! + 1$ is divided by r, where $1 < r \leq n$, there is a remainder of 1. Indeed, one has that

$$(n! + 1)/r = n!/r + 1/r$$

Hence $n! + 1$ has no prime factor between 1 and n. But by assumption, it has a prime factor.

Hence the prime factor is greater than n, which contradicts the assumption that n is the largest prime number.

Proof. Assume, to the contrary, that there are a finite number of primes. Let n be the largest prime. Then n! + 1 is not a prime since, n! + 1 > n. Therefore, n! + 1 has a prime factor p less than or equal to n. But n! + 1 cannot be divided by any number between 1 and n. Hence p > n and we therefore arrive at a contradiction.//

8.9. (a) Construction method is to be used.
Construct an element s in S and show that s is in T.
(b) Choose and contradiction methods, in that order.
Choose s' in S and conclude that there is no t in T such that s' > t. To reach the conclusion, use the contradiction method to assume that there is a t in T such that s' > t. Now reach a contradiction.
(c) Contradiction method is to be used.
Assume that there exists an M > 0 such that, for all x in S, |x| < M, and try to reach a contradiction.

Chapter 9

9.1. (a) Work forward from: n is an odd integer.
Try to conclude: n^2 is an odd integer.
(b) Work forward from: S is a subset of T, and T is bounded.
Try to conclude: S is bounded.
(c) Work forward from: f(x) = f(y).
Try to conclude: x = y.
(d) Work forward from: the rows of matrix M are linearly dependent.
Try to conclude: M is singular.

9.2. Statement (b) is a result of the forward process because you can assume that there is a real number t between 0 and $\pi/4$ such that $\sin(t) = r \cos(t)$. Upon squaring both sides, the answer in part (b) results.

9.3. To use the contrapositive method, we need to work forward from NOT B and backward from NOT A.
   (a) Incorrect, the abstraction process should not be applied to NOT B. This abstraction question also contains specific notation from the problem.
   (b) Incorrect, because the abstraction question contains specific notation from the problem.
   (c) Incorrect, because the abstraction process should not be applied to NOT B.
   (d) Correct.

9.4. Outline of proof. With the contrapositive method, one can assume that there is an odd integer solution, say m, to the equation $n^2 + n - c = 0$. It must be shown that c is not odd, i.e., that c is even. But from the equation, one can write that $c = m + m^2$. To see that c is even, observe that m is odd, and so m^2 is also odd (see Exercise 3.5). Hence $c = m + m^2 = $ odd $+$ odd $=$ even, and the proof is complete.

   Proof. Assume that there is an odd integer solution, say m, to the equation $n^2 + n - c = 0$. It will be shown that c is not odd. But $c = m + m^2$, and since m is odd, $m + m^2$ is even, and so c is even.//

9.5. Outline of proof. The appearance of the quantifier "for all" in the conclusion suggests using the choose method, whereby one chooses real numbers x and y with $x \neq y$, for which it must be shown that

   B1: $f(x) \neq f(y)$.

   The word "not" in B1 now suggests proceeding with the contradiction or contrapositive method. Here, the contrapositive method will be used,

and accordingly, it can be assumed that
f(x) = f(y). Now it must be shown that x = y.
To reach the desired conclusion, work forward
from the fact that f(x) = f(y). Specifically,
mx + b = my + b, and subtracting the right side
from both sides of the equation, one obtains
m(x - y) = 0. Using the hypothesis that m ≠ 0,
it follows that x - y = 0, and consequently
x = y.

Proof. Assume that x and y are real numbers for
which f(x) = f(y). It will be shown that x = y.
But since f(x) = f(y), it then follows that
mx + b = my + b, or, m(x - y) = 0. By the
hypothesis that m ≠ 0, one reaches the desired
conclusion that x = y.//

9.6. Outline of proof. By the contrapositive method,
one can assume that the quadrilateral RSTU is
not a rectangle. It must be shown that there is
an obtuse angle. The appearance of the
quantifier "there is" suggests turning to the
forward process to produce the desired obtuse
angle.

Working forward, one can conclude that at
least one angle of the quadriateral is not 90
degrees, say it is angle R. If angle R has more
than 90 degrees, then it is the desired angle.
Otherwise, angle R has less than 90 degrees.
This, in turn, means that the remaining angles
of the quadrilateral must add up to more than
270 degrees (because the sum of all the angles
in RSTU is 360 degrees). Among these three
angles that add up to more than 270 degrees, one
of them must be greater than 90 degrees, and
that is the desired obtuse angle.

Proof. Assume that the quadrilateral RSTU is
not a rectangle, and hence, one of its angles,
say R, is not 90 degrees. An obtuse angle will
be found. If angle R has more than 90 degrees,
then it is the desired angle. Otherwise, the
remaining three angles add up to more than 270
degrees. Therefore, one of the remaining three
angles is obtuse.//

Chapter 10

10.1. (a) The real number x^* is not a maximum of the function f if there is a real number. x such that $f(x) > f(x^*)$.

(b) Suppose that f and g are functions of one variable. Then g is not $\geq$ f on the set S of real numbers if there exists an element x in S such that $g(x) < f(x)$.

(c) The real number u is not an upper bound for a set S of real numbers if there exists an x in S such that $x > u$.

(d) The real number u is not a least upper bound for a set S of real numbers if u is not an upper bound for S, or if there exists a real number $\varepsilon > 0$ such that for all x in S, $x \leq u - \varepsilon$.

(e) The set C of real numbers is not convex if there exist elements x and y in C and there exists a real number t between zero and one such that $tx + (1 - t)y$ is not an element of C.

(f) The function f of one variable is not convex if there exist real numbers x and y and t, where $0 \leq t \leq 1$, such that $f(tx + (1 - t)y) > tf(x) + (1 - t)f(y)$.

(g) The function f of one variable is not continuous at the point x if there exists real number $\varepsilon > 0$ such that for all real numbers $\delta > 0$, there is a y with $|x - y| < \delta$ such that $|f(x) - f(y)| \geq \varepsilon$.

(h) Suppose that $x, x^1, x^2, \ldots$ are real numbers. The sequence $x^1, x^2, \ldots$ does not converge to x if $\exists$ a real number $\varepsilon > 0$ $\ni$ $\forall$ integers k', $\exists$ an integer $k > k'$ such that $|x^k - x| \geq \varepsilon$.

10.2. (a) There does not exist an element x in the set S such that x is not in T.

(b) It is not true that for every angle t between 0 and $\pi/2$, $\sin(t) \neq \cos(t)$.

(c) There does not exist an "object" with the "certain property" such that the "something" does not happen.

(d) It is not true that for every "object" with the "certain property," the "something" does not happen.

10.3. (a) Assume that there is an integer $n \geq 4$ such that $n! \leq n^2$.

(b) Assume A, NOT B AND NOT C.

(c) Assume A, NOT B OR NOT C.

(d) Assume that f is a convex function of one variable, x^* is a real number, and there is a real number $\delta > 0$ such that for all real numbers x with the property that $|x - x^*| < \delta$, $f(x) \geq f(x^*)$. Finally, assume that there is a real number y such that $f(y) < f(x^*)$.

10.4. (a) Forward from: (NOT B) AND (NOT C)
        Backward from: NOT A

(b) Forward from: (NOT B) OR (NOT C)
    Backward from: NOT A

(c) Forward from: mn is not divisible by 4 and n is divisible by 4.
    Backward from: n is an odd integer or m is an even integer.

10.5. Outline of proof. When using the contradiction method, it can be assumed that $x \geq 0$, $y \geq 0$, $x + y = 0$, and that either $x \neq 0$ or $y \neq 0$. So suppose first that $x \neq 0$ and hence, since $x \geq 0$, it must be that $x > 0$. A contradiction to the fact that $y \geq 0$ will be reached by showing that $y < 0$. Specifically, since $x + y = 0$, it follows that $y = -x$ but $-x < 0$ and so the contradiction has been reached. A similar argument can be used for the case where $y \neq 0$.

Proof. Assume that $x \geq 0$, $y \geq 0$, $x + y = 0$, and that either $x \neq 0$ or $y \neq 0$. If $x \neq 0$, then $x > 0$ and $y = -x < 0$, but this contradicts the fact that $y \geq 0$. Similarly, if $y \neq 0$, then $y > 0$, and $x = -y < 0$, but this contradicts the fact that $x \geq 0$.//

Chapter 11

11.1. Outline of proof. The first uniqueness method
will be used, wherein one must first construct
the real number y. This, however, was already
done in Exercise 5.7. Thus, it remains only to
show the uniqueness by assuming that y and z
are both real numbers with $y < 0$, $z < 0$,
$x = 2y/(1 + y)$, and $x = 2z/(1 + z)$. By working
forward via algebraic manipulations, it will be
shown that $y = z$. Specifically,

$$x = 2y/(1 + y) = 2z/(1 + z)$$

or equivalently,

$$y + yz = z + yz$$

and, on subtracting yz from both sides, one
obtains the desired conclusion that $y = z$.//

Proof. The existence of the real number y was
established in Exercise 5.7. To show that y is
unique, suppose that y and z satisfy $y < 0$,
$z < 0$, $x = 2y/(1 + y)$, and $x = 2z/(1 + z)$. But
then it follows that $2y/(1 + y) = 2z/(1 + z)$,
and so $y + yz = z + yz$, or, $y = z$, as
desired.//

11.2. Outline of proof. According to the second
uniqueness method, we must first construct a
real number x for which $mx + b = 0$. But since
the hypothesis states the $m \neq 0$, the desired x
is $-b/m$, because then it follows that
$mx + b = m(-b/m) + b = -b + b = 0$.

To establish the uniqueness, suppose that
x and y both satisfy $mx + b = 0$ and $my + b = 0$,
and also that $x \neq y$. A contradiction is
reached by showing that $m = 0$. Specifically,
since $mx + b = 0 = my + b$, it follows that
$m(x - y) = 0$. On dividing by the nonzero
number $x - y$, it follows that $m = 0$.

Proof. To construct the number x for which
mx + b = 0, let x = -b/m (noting that m ≠ 0).
Then mx + b = m(-b/m) + b = 0.

Now suppose that y ≠ x and also satisfies
my + b = 0. Then mx + b = my + b, and so
m(x - y) = 0. But since x - y ≠ 0, it must be
that m = 0, and this contradicts the hypothesis
that m ≠ 0.//

11.3. Outline of proof. The issue of existence must
be addressed first. To construct the desired
complex number (c + di) that satisfies
(a + bi)(c + di) = 1, let c = a/(a^2 + b^2) and
d = -b/(a^2 + b^2) (noting that the denominator
is not 0 since, by the hypothesis, at least one
of a or b is not 0). But then,

(a + bi)(c + di) = ac - bd + (bc + ad)i

$$= (a^2 + b^2)/(a^2 + b^2) + 0i$$

$$= 1.$$

To see the uniqueness, suppose that e + fi
is another complex number that also satisfies
(a + bi)(e + fi) = 1. It will be shown that
c + di equals e + fi. Working forward and
multiplying both sides of the equation above by
e + fi, one obtains:

(e + fi)[(a + bi)(c + di)] = (e + fi)(1),
or,
[(e + fi)(a + bi)](c + di) = e + fi,

and since (e + fi)(a + bi) = 1, it follows that
c + di = e + fi.

Proof. Since either a ≠ 0 or b ≠ 0, it follows
that a^2 + b^2 ≠ 0, and so it is possible to
construct the complex number c + di in which
c = a/(a^2 + b^2) and d = -b/(a^2 + b^2), for then

(a + bi)(c + di) = ac - bd + (bc + ad)i

$$= 1.$$

To see the uniqueness, suppose that e + fi also satisfies (a + bi)(e + fi) = 1. By the rules of complex multiplication, it follows that

$$(e + fi)[(a + bi)(c + di)] = (e + fi)(1)$$

so c + di = e + fi and the uniqueness is established.//

11.4. Advantages: You have three statements to work forward from, namely, A, NOT B, and NOT C. With the either/or method, you would only have two statements to work forward from.

Disadvantages: You cannot work backward because you do not know what the contradiction will be. In the either/or method you can work backward from the statement (B OR C).

11.5. Outline of proof. By the either/or method, we can assume that n is an even integer and m is and odd integer, and also that 4 divides n. We must conclude that 4 divides mn.

Working backward, one is led to the abstraction question "How can I show one integer (namely 4) divides another (namely mn)?" Using the definition leads to the answer that one must show that there is an integer k such that mn = 4k.

Turning to the forward process, we must construct the value for k. Since m is odd, there is an integer j such that m = 2j + 1. Since 4 divides n, there is and integer p such that n = 4p. Therefore

$$mn = (2j + 1)(4p) = 4(2jp + p)$$

and the desired k is k = 2jp + p.

Proof. Assume that n is even, m is odd, and that 4 divides n. It will be shown that 4 divides mn, or equivalently, that there is an integer k such that mn = 4k. But since m is odd, there is an integer j such that m = 2j + 1. Since 4 divides n, there is and integer p such that n = 4p. Thus,

mn = (2j + 1)(4p) = 4(2jp + p).

Hence, the desired integer is k = 2jp + p, thus completing the proof.//

Note: This proof could also be done by assuming n is an even integer and m is an odd integer, and that 4 does not divide mn, and then concluding that 4 does not divide n.

11.6. (a) If x is a real number that satisfies $x^3 + 3x^2 - 9x - 27 \geq 0$, then x ≤ -3 or x ≥ 3.

(b) Outline of proof. According to the either/or method, we can assume that $x^3 + 3x^2 - 9x - 27 \geq 0$ and that x > -3. We must show that x ≥ 3. Now one has

$$x^3 + 3x^2 - 9x - 27 = (x - 3)(x + 3)^2 \geq 0.$$

Since x > -3, $(x + 3)^2$ is positive, and so we must have x - 3 ≥ 0, or, x ≥ 3.

Proof. Assume that $x^3 + 3x^2 - 9x - 27 \geq 0$ and that x > -3. Then it follows that

$$x^3 + 3x^2 - 9x - 27 = (x - 3)(x + 3)^2 \geq 0.$$

Since x > -3, $(x + 3)^2$ is positive, so x - 3 ≥ 0, or equivalently, x ≥ 3.//

(c) The proof is similar to part (b) except you assume that x < 3.

11.7. (a) For all s in S, s ≤ x.

(b) There is an s in S such that s ≥ x.

(c) There is an x with ax ≤ b and x ≥ 0 such that cx ≤ u.

(d) There is an x with ax $\geq$ b and x $\geq$ 0 such that cx $\geq$ u.

(e) For all x with b $\leq$ x $\leq$ c, ax $\geq$ u.

(f) For all x with a $\leq$ x $\leq$ c, bx $\leq$ u.

11.8. Outline of proof. The max/min method can be used to convert the conclusion into the equivalent quantifier statement:

B: for all s in S, s $\geq$ t*.

The appearance of the quantifier "for all" in the backward process suggests using the choose method to choose an s' in S, for which it must be shown that

B1: s' $\geq$ t*.

The desired conclusion can be obtained by working forward and using specialization. Specifically, since S is a subset of T, it follows that

A1: for all s in S, s is in T.

Specializing A1 to s = s' (which is in S), it follows that s' is in T. Also, the hypothesis states that

A2: for all t in T, t $\geq$ t*.

Again, applying specialization to A2 with t = s' (which is in T), it follows that s' $\geq$ t*, and thus the proof is complete.

Proof. To reach the conclusion, let s' be in S. It will be shown that s' $\geq$ t*. By the hypothesis that S is a subset of T, it follow that s' is in T. But then, the hypothesis ensures that s' $\geq$ t*.//

11.9. Outline of proof. The max/min method can be used to convert the conclusion into the equivalent quantifier statement:

B1: for all x ≥ 0 with ax ≥ b, and for all
u ≥ 0 with ua ≤ c, cx ≥ ub.

The appearance of the quantifier "for all" in
the backward process suggests choosing an
x' ≥ 0 with ax' ≥ b, and also choosing u' ≥ 0
with u'a ≤ c, for which it must be shown that
cx' ≥ u'b. To accomplish the goal, it will be
shown that cx' ≥ u'ax' and that u'ax' ≥ u'b.
Specifically, upon multiplying both sides of
the inequality u'a ≤ c by the nonnegative
number x', it follows that cx' ≥ u'ax'.
Similarly, upon multiplying the inequality
ax' ≥ b on both sides by the nonnegative number
u', it follows that u'ax' ≥ u'b, and the proof
is complete.

Proof. To reach the desired conclusion, let
x' ≥ 0 with ax' ≥ b, and let u' ≥ 0 with
u'a ≤ c. It then follows that u'ax' ≥ u'b and
cx' ≥ u'ax', and therefore one has that
cx' ≥ u'ax' ≥ u'b, and consequently the proof
is complete.//

Chapter 12

12.1. (a) Contrapositive or contradiction method,
         since the word "no" appears in the
         conclusion.
     (b) Induction method, since statement B is true
         for every integer n ≥ 4.
     (c) Forward-Backward method, since there is no
         apparent form to B.
     (d) Max/min method, since B has the word
         "maximum" in it.
     (e) Uniqueness method, since there is supposed
         to be one and only one line.
     (f) Contradiction or contrapositive method,
         since the word "no" appears in the
         conclusion.

(g) Forward-Backward method, since there is no apparent form to B.

(h) Choose method, since the first quantifier in B is "for every."

(i) Construction method, since the first quantifier in B is "there is."

12.2. (a) Using the induction method, we would assume $n! > n^2$ and $n \geq 4$, and try to show that $(n + 1)! > (n + 1)^2$. We would, of course, also have to show that $4! > 4^2$.

(b) Using the choose method, we would choose an integer n' for which $n' \geq 4$. We would try to show that $(n')! > (n')^2$.

(c) Converting the statement to the form "if . . . then . . . " one obtains "if n is an integer ≥ 4 then $n! > n^2$". We would therefore assume that n is an integer ≥ 4 and try to show that $n! > n^2$.

(d) Using the contradiction method, we would assume that there is an integer $n \geq 4$ such that $n! \leq n^2$, and try to reach a contradiction.

Glossary of Mathematical Symbols

Symbol	Meaning	Page
=>	implies	3
<=> (iff)	if and only if	26
$\in$	is an element of	40
$\subseteq$	subset	42
$\emptyset$	empty set	42
$\sim$	not	30
$\forall$	for all (for each, etc.)	43
$\exists$	there is (there are, etc.)	36
$\ni$	such that	36
$\wedge$	and	24
$\vee$	or	24
Q.E.D.	*quod erat demonstrandum* (which was to be demonstrated)	14

index

INSTRUCTOR'S SURVEY
How to Read and Do Proofs

Completion of the following information will assist in the evaluation and modification of this pamphlet. Please complete, fold, staple, and mail. Your comments are appreciated.

Name _____

Department _____

University _____

1. Title of course for which pamphlet was assigned

_____

2. Approximate class enrollment _____

3. Level of the course
_____ undergraduate _____ graduate

4. How the pamphlet was used
_____ required _____ recommended

5. Were the proof techniques useful in teaching the course material? _____ yes _____ no

6. Did your class lectures include a discussion of the individual proof techniques?
_____ yes—approximate number of hours devoted to
it _____
_____ no

7. When proofs were taught in class, was specific reference made to the techniques? _____ yes _____ no

8. Suggestions for improving the pamphlet.

_____

_____

_____

_____

solow/proofs/0 471 86645 8